To all children
who love to read, color,
and keep their room clean!

First published by Mrs.D.Books LLC

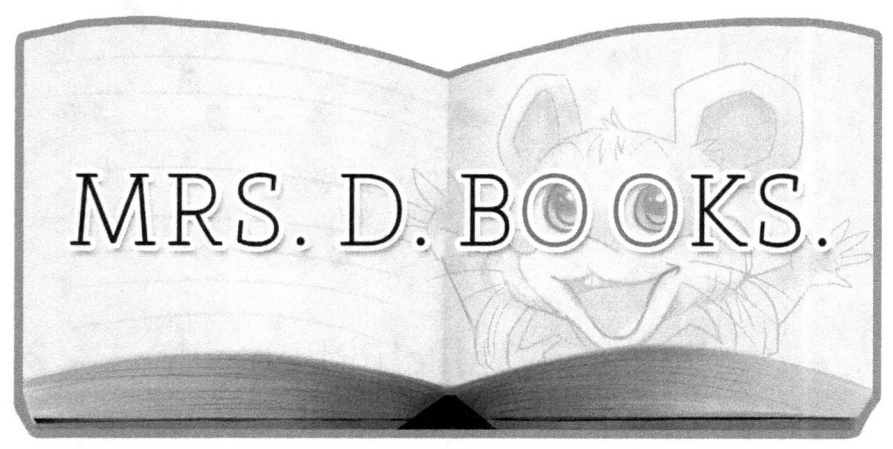

ISBN 978-1981925322

To order additional paperback or hardcover copies
of "Runaway Clothes," or this book, please
visit Amazon.com, Barnesandnoble.com, or
the author's website, www.mrsdbooks.net, or
email olga@mrsdbooks.com.

E-book versions are also available
through Amazon, Barnes and Noble,
and Apple.

All about _____

I am _____ years old. I have _____ hair

and _____ eyes.

My birthday is on _____.

My favorite toy is _____.

These are a few of my
favorite
things

Color _____
Food _____
Animal _____
Book _____
Clothes _____
Game _____

Runaway Clothes

An enlightening story about a little girl named Nika who didn't want to take care of her clothes and toys. One hazy morning when Nika opened her closet, she discovered that it was empty. Her clothes had disappeared! What had happened to her shirts and pants? Where did her favorite dresses, coats, and socks go? Why did they leave her with just her pajamas on this misty morning? Will they come back? Taking a closer look at her room, Nika starts thinking about her attitude toward her clothes and toys. "How easy it is to lose something you love so much." She learns an important lesson at the end of this story. Watch your children have a blast reading this story while learning valuable lessons.

Preface

Do you have a young lady in your home who is a less than perfect housekeeper? "Runaway Clothes" is just what the doctor ordered!

We've all been there with our kids... cluttered desks, things on the floor, boxes under the bed, clutter on the shelves, messy closets, and rooms looking as if a tornado had just traveled through them. How many times have we told our youngsters that if they do not clean their room, something bad might happen? They just smirked, gave us a strange look, or simply ignored our warnings.

"Just wait!" We bite our lips, not having any idea how to replace the cutest smirks on their faces with an ugly fear. Some of us gave up and let them drown in their own mess, but some like me were determined to find the solution to the messy room.

Often, children learn lessons when we least expect them. That was what happened to my young heroine in my multi-award-winning children's book "Runaway Clothes." This book was based on an event that happened in my home many years ago...

I hope your little ones will enjoy the beautiful artwork in this full-of-activities coloring book, while having fun decorating clothing and writing their own story. They can compare their artwork to the original art in the printed book, "Runaway Clothes." If you wish to get the autographed book, which includes a special message for your child, please visit Mrs. D's Store on Etsy. I would be happy to read your reviews, and if you send your children's stories to olga@mrsdbooks.com I will gladly post them on Mrs. D's Blog with your permission. Happy reading and coloring!

Mrs. D ~

Match the clothing!

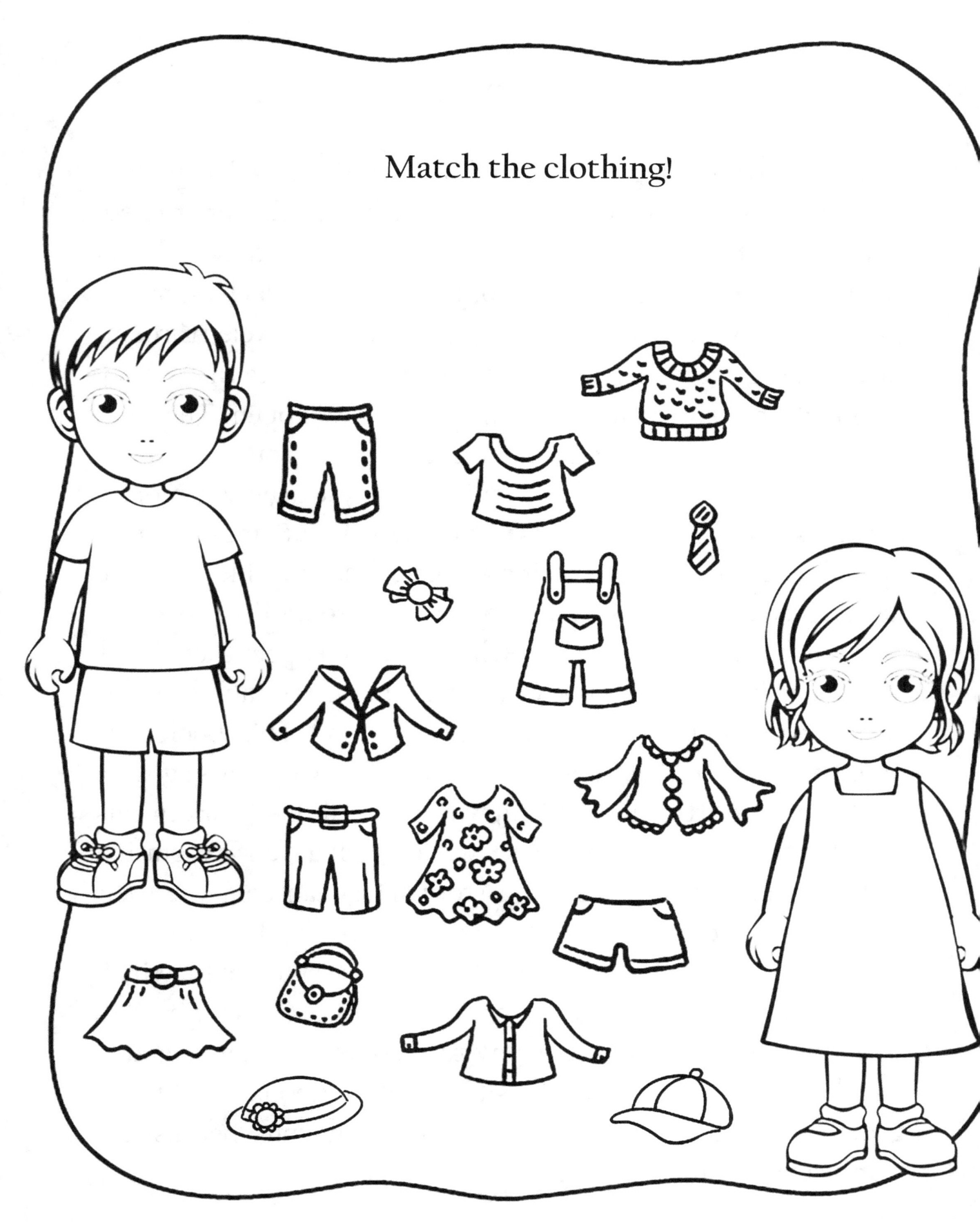

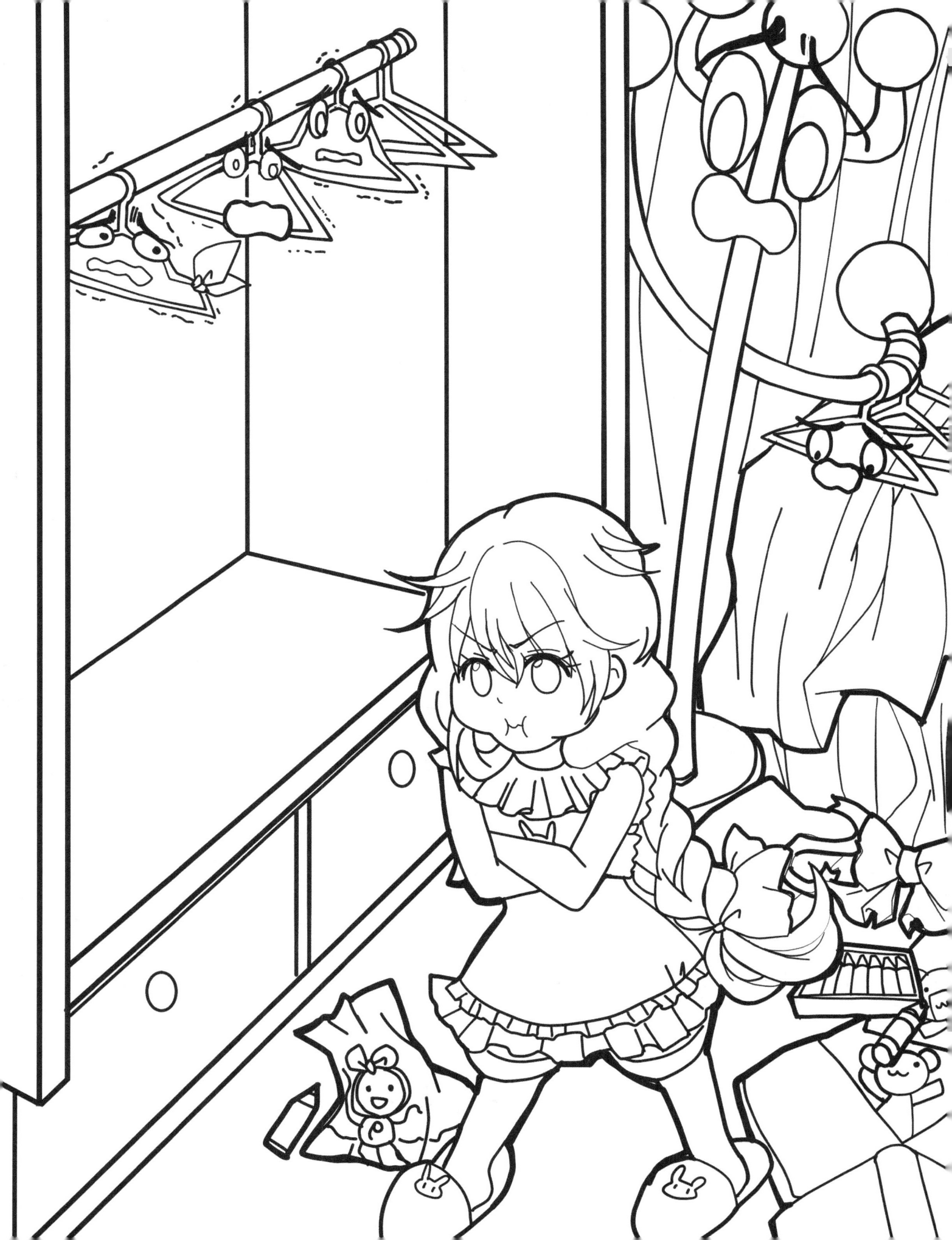

Match the toys' names to the right picture and color them.

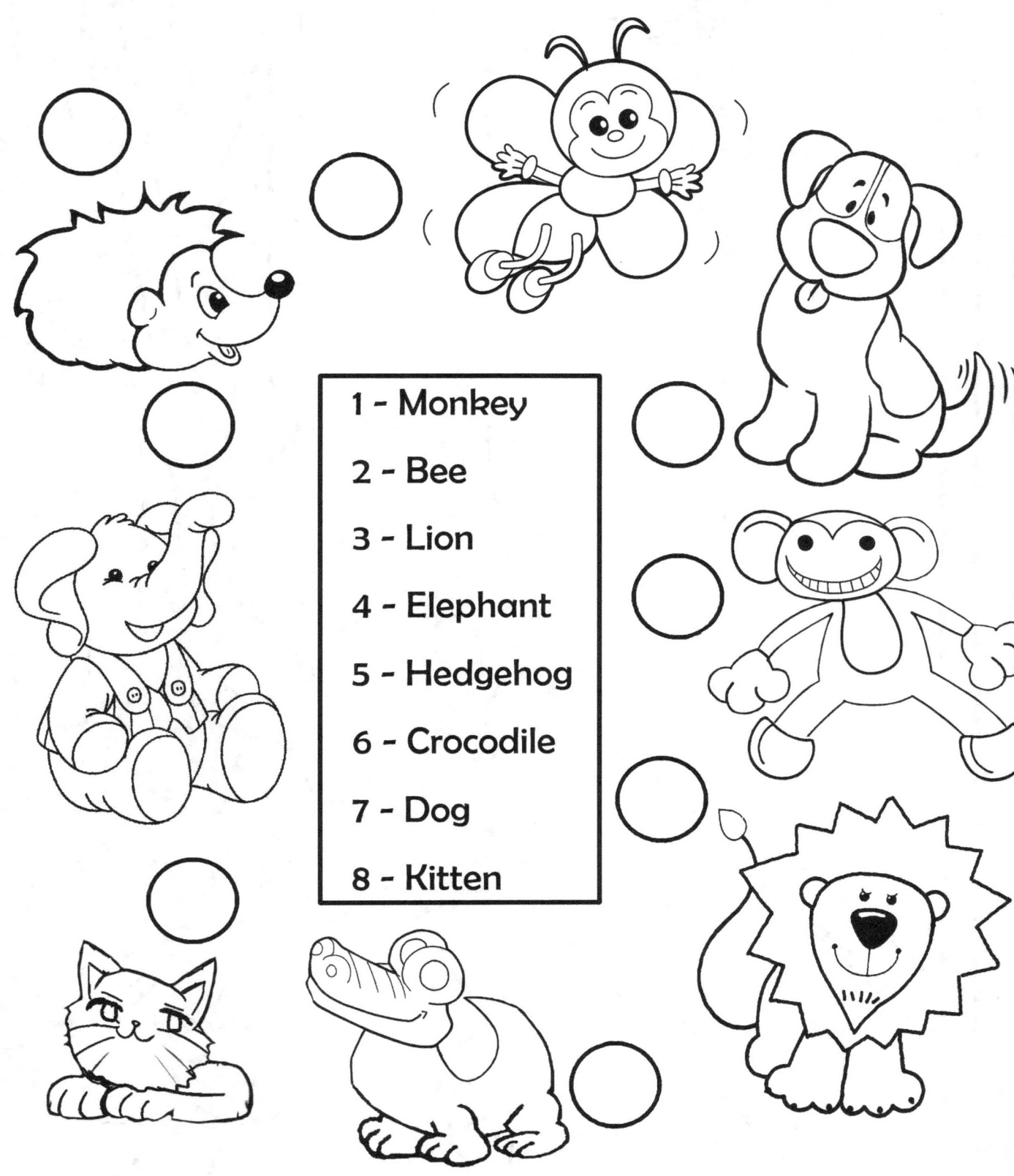

1 - Monkey

2 - Bee

3 - Lion

4 - Elephant

5 - Hedgehog

6 - Crocodile

7 - Dog

8 - Kitten

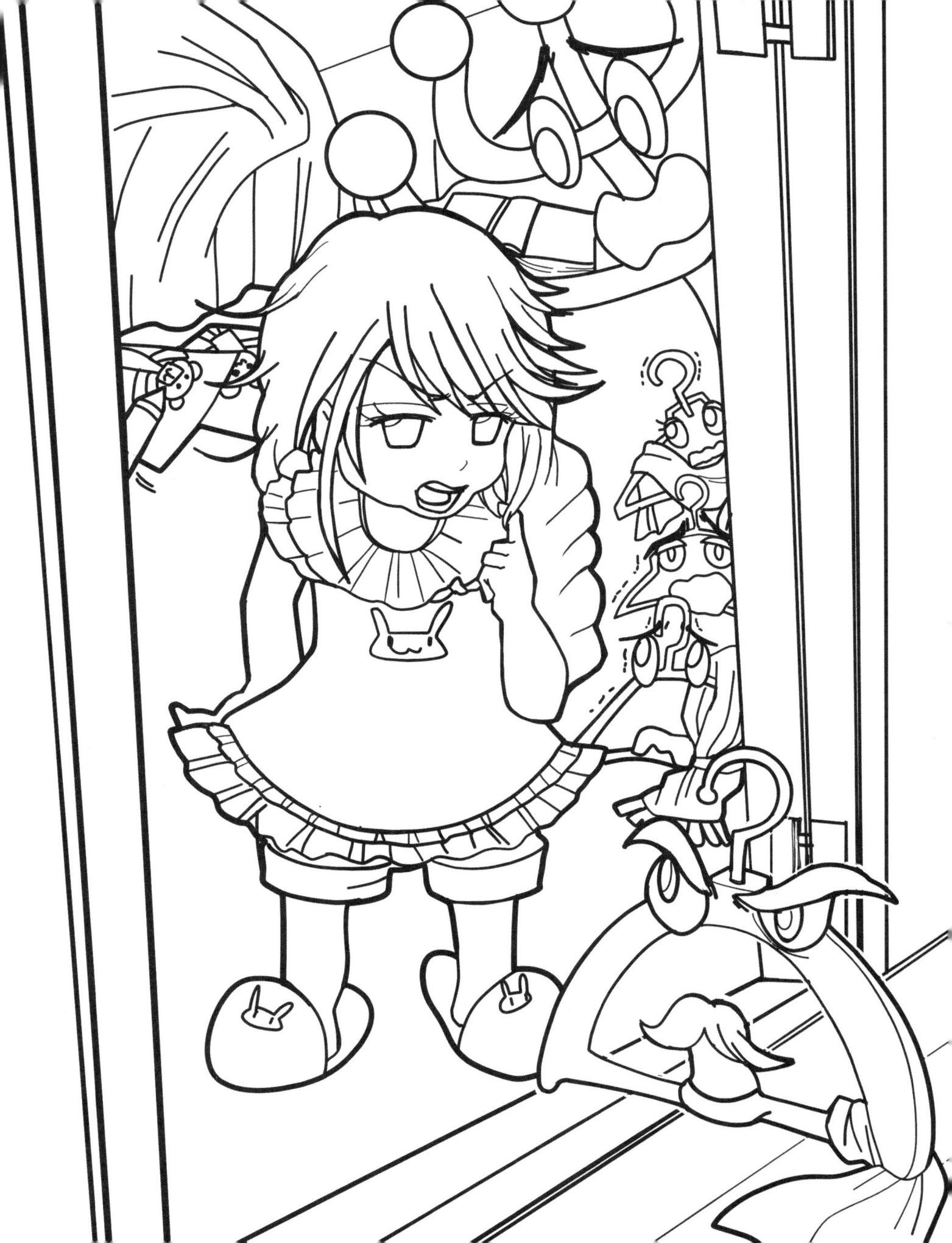

Find three roads to the flowers!
Color the sunbeam and flowers!

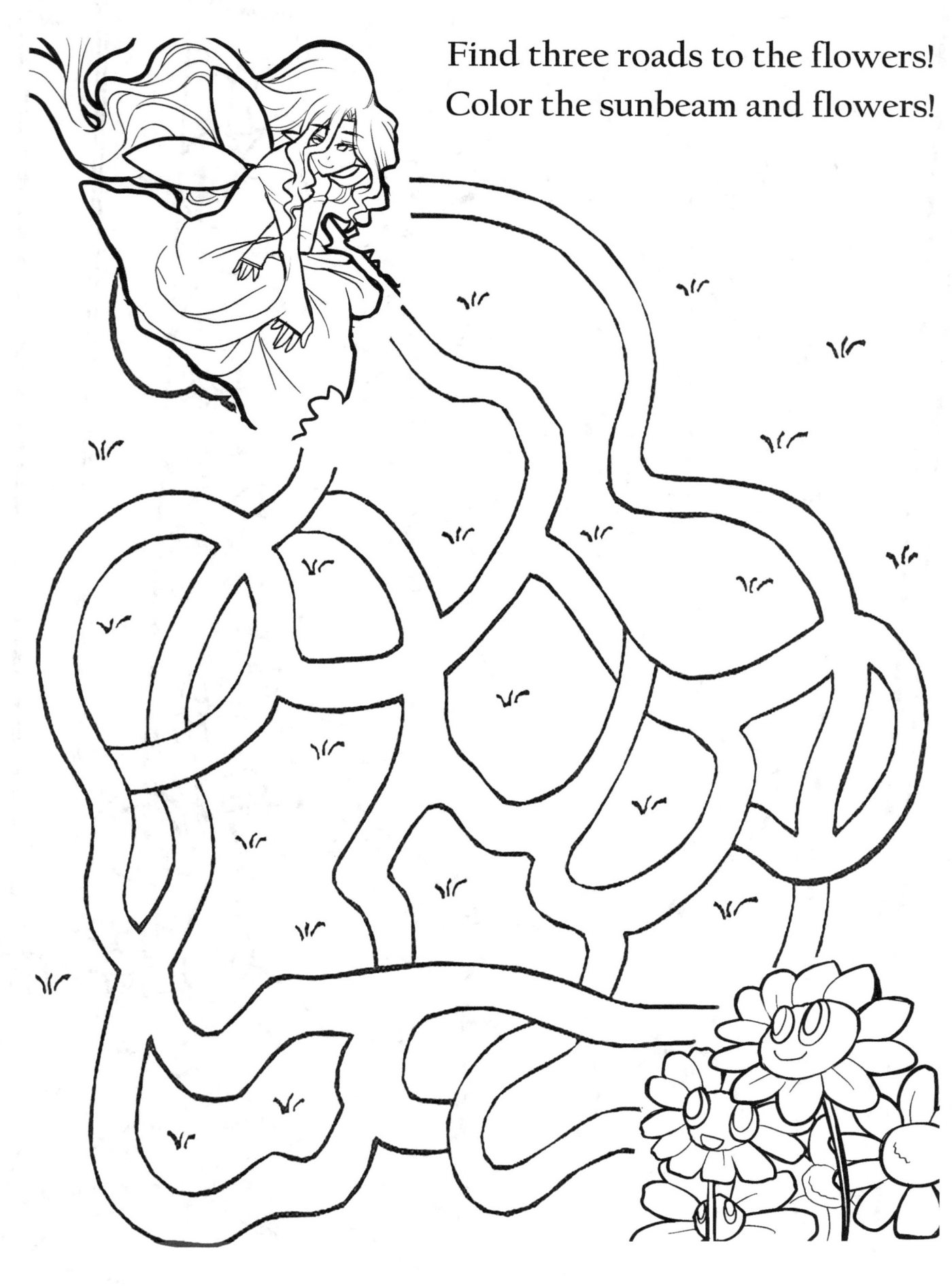

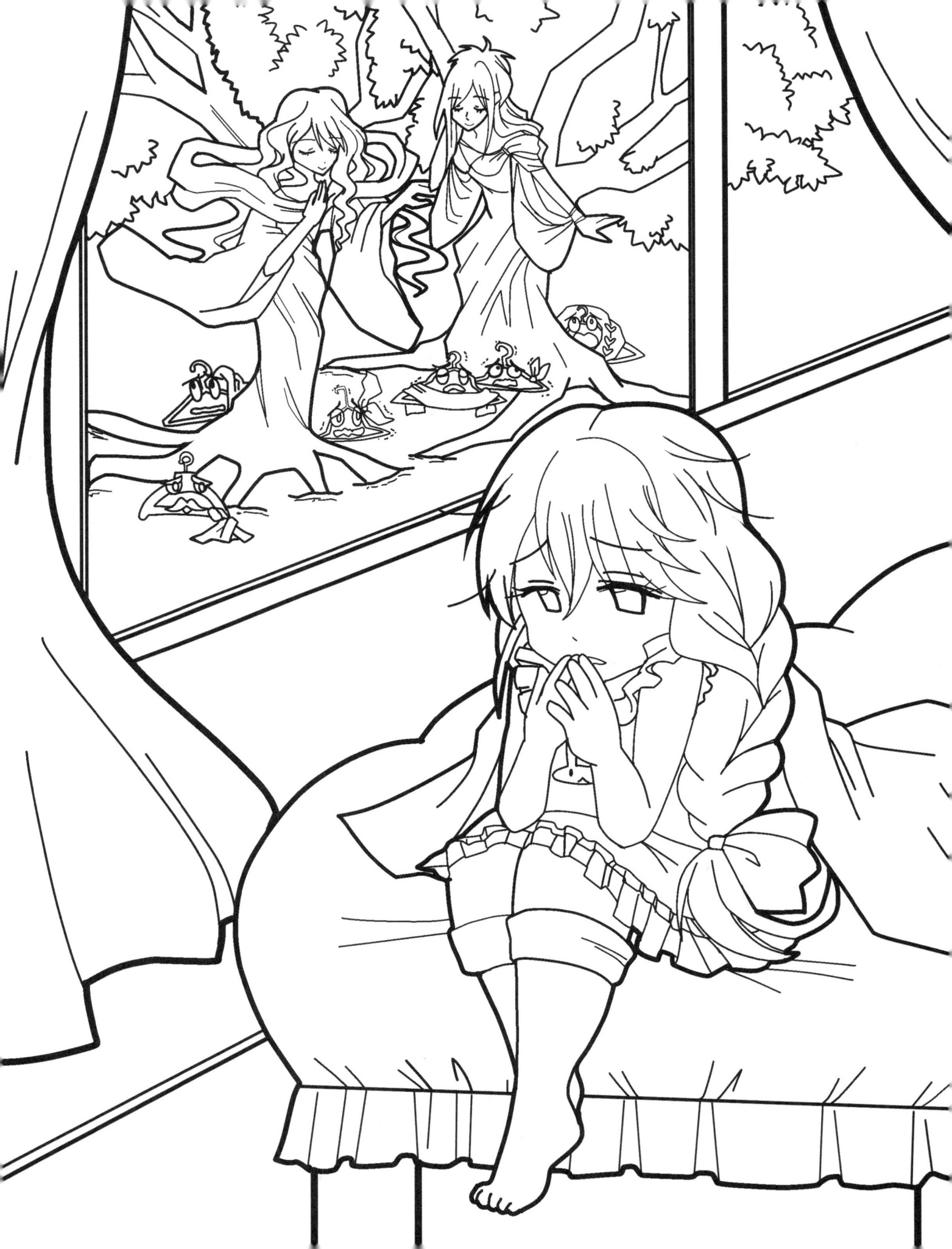

Dress the little people according to the weather: spring, summer, autumn, winter!

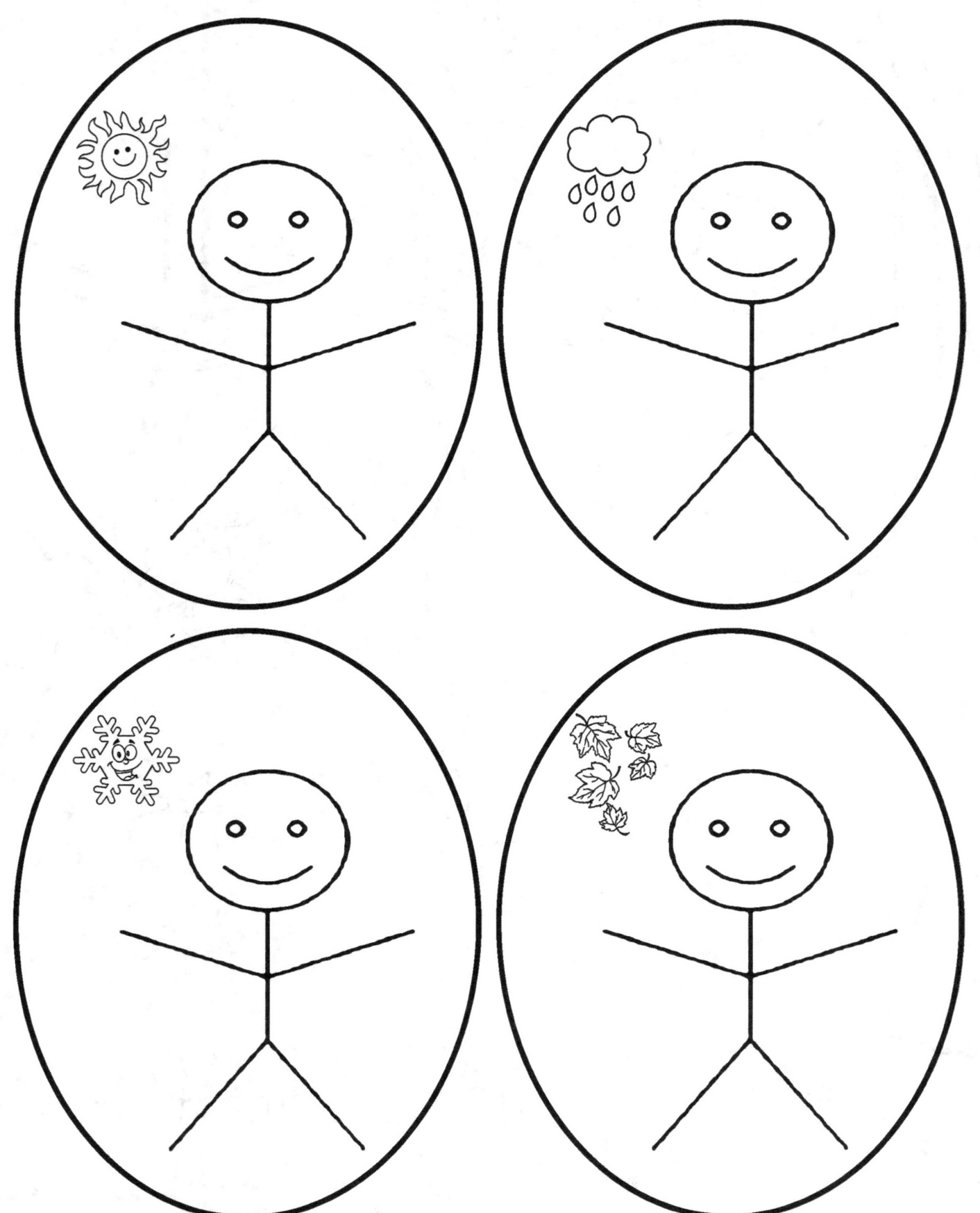

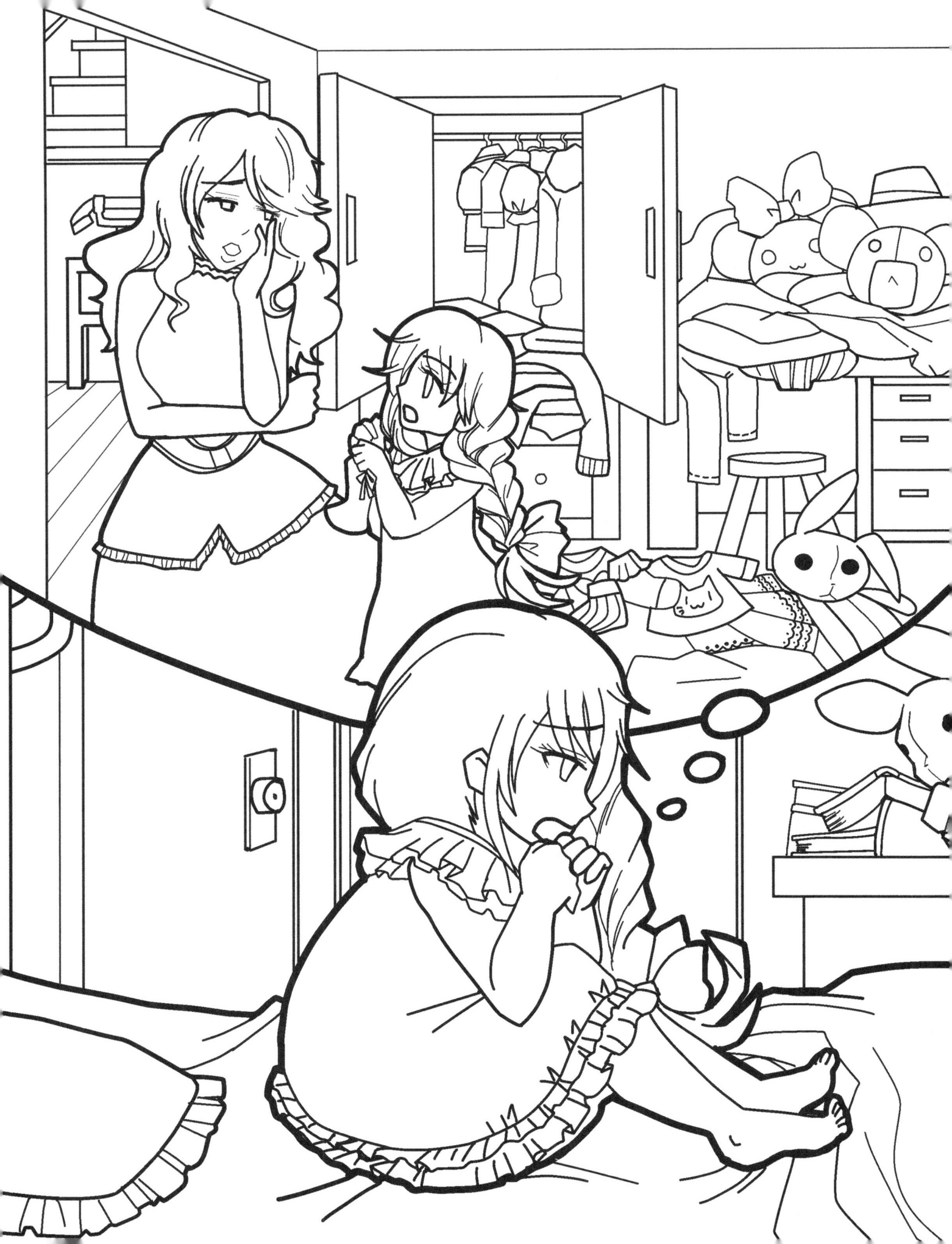

Fill in the missing letter!

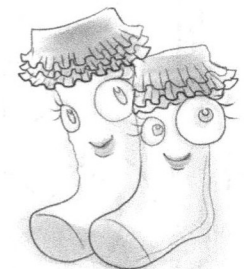

S _ _ _ _ _

P _ _ _ _ _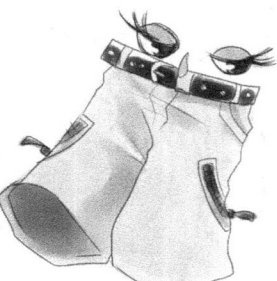

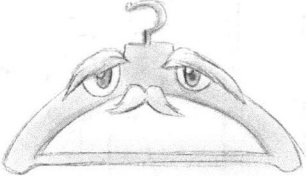 H _ _ _ _ _

S _ _ _ _ _ _ _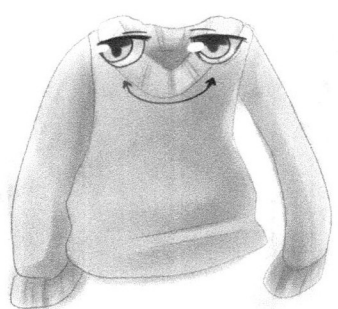

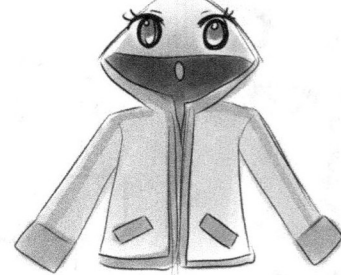 J _ _ _ _ _

C _ _ _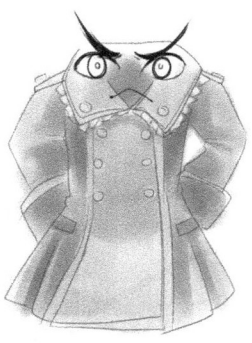

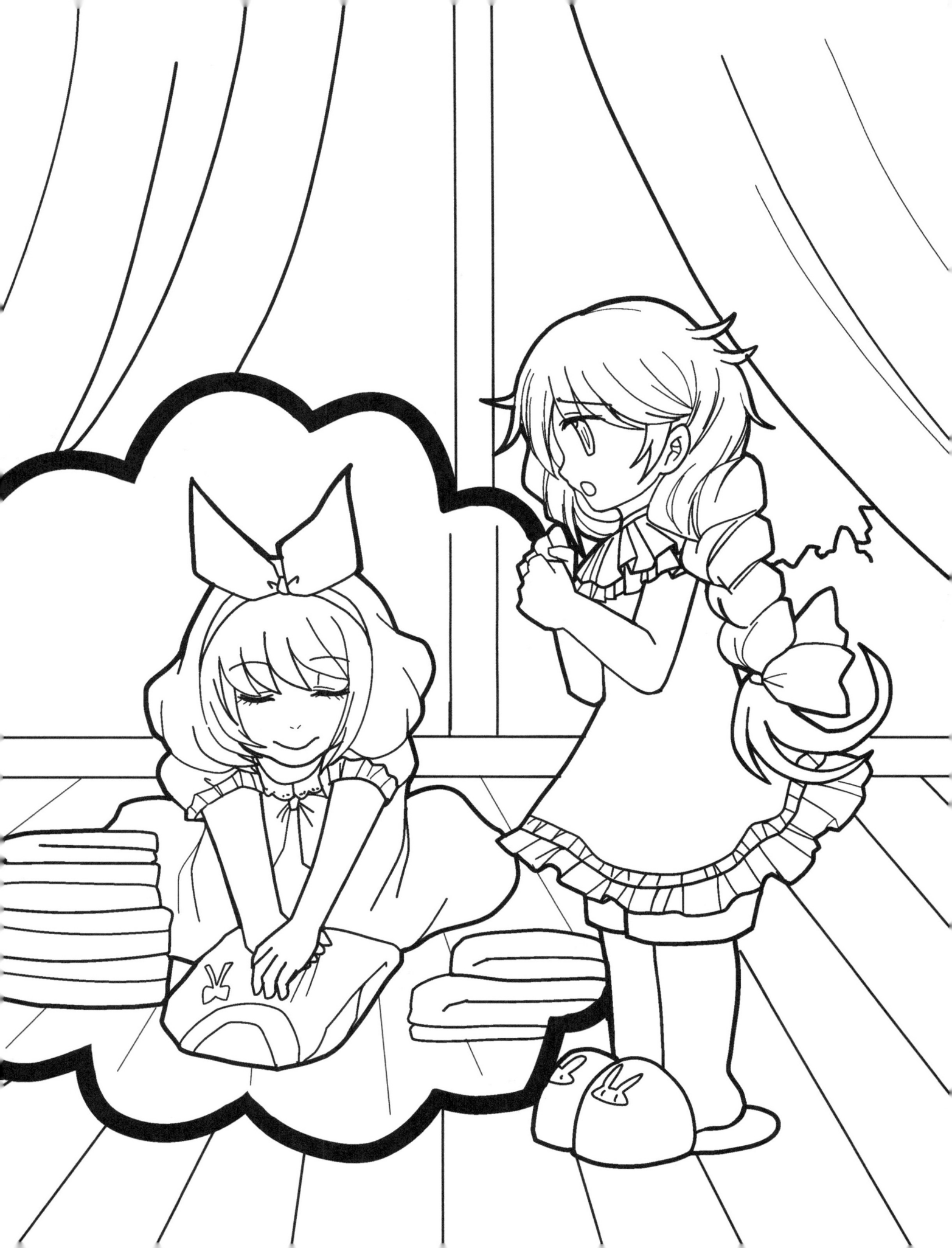

Finish this drawing: connect all dots!

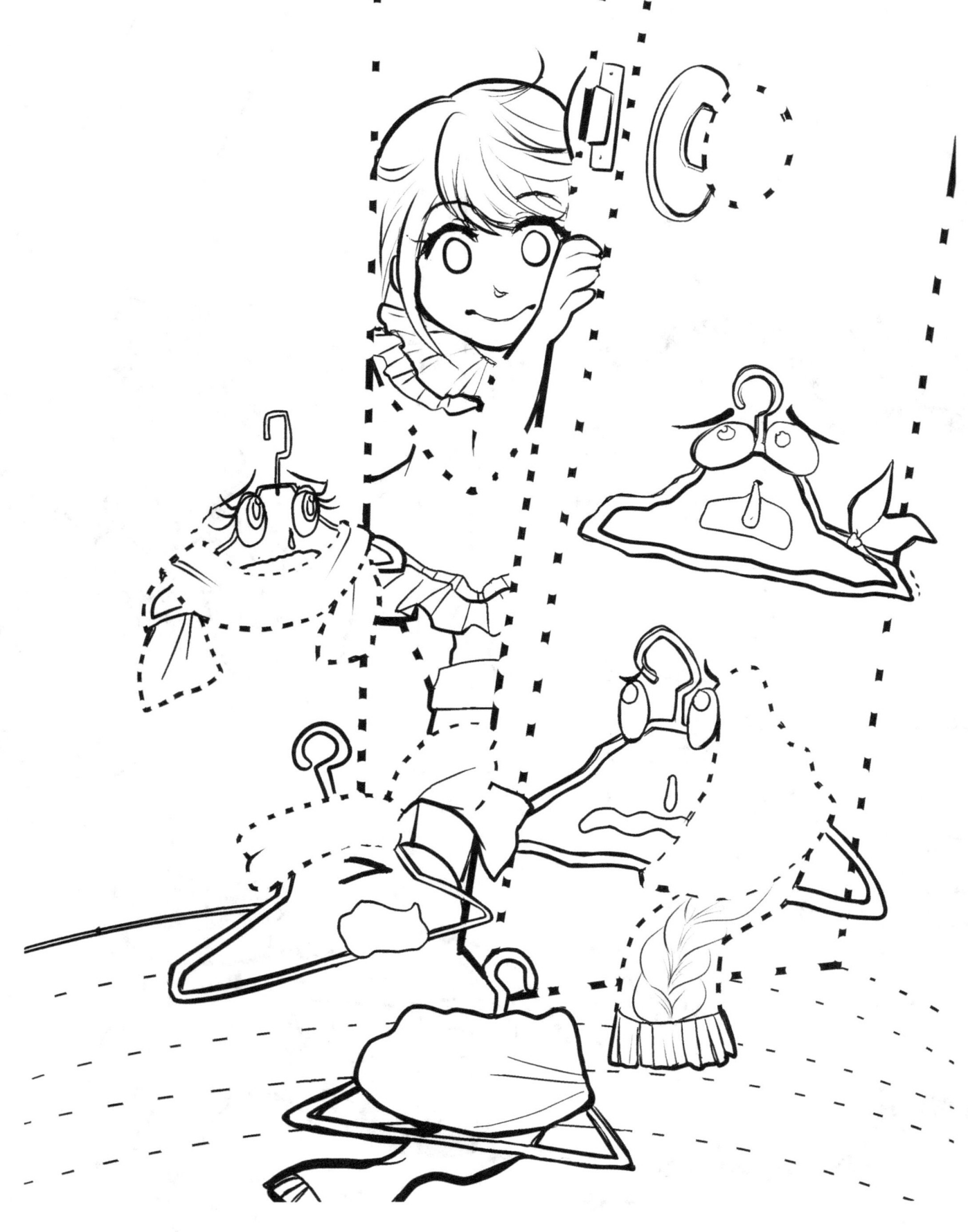

Connect dots and find the string leading the hanger to Nika!

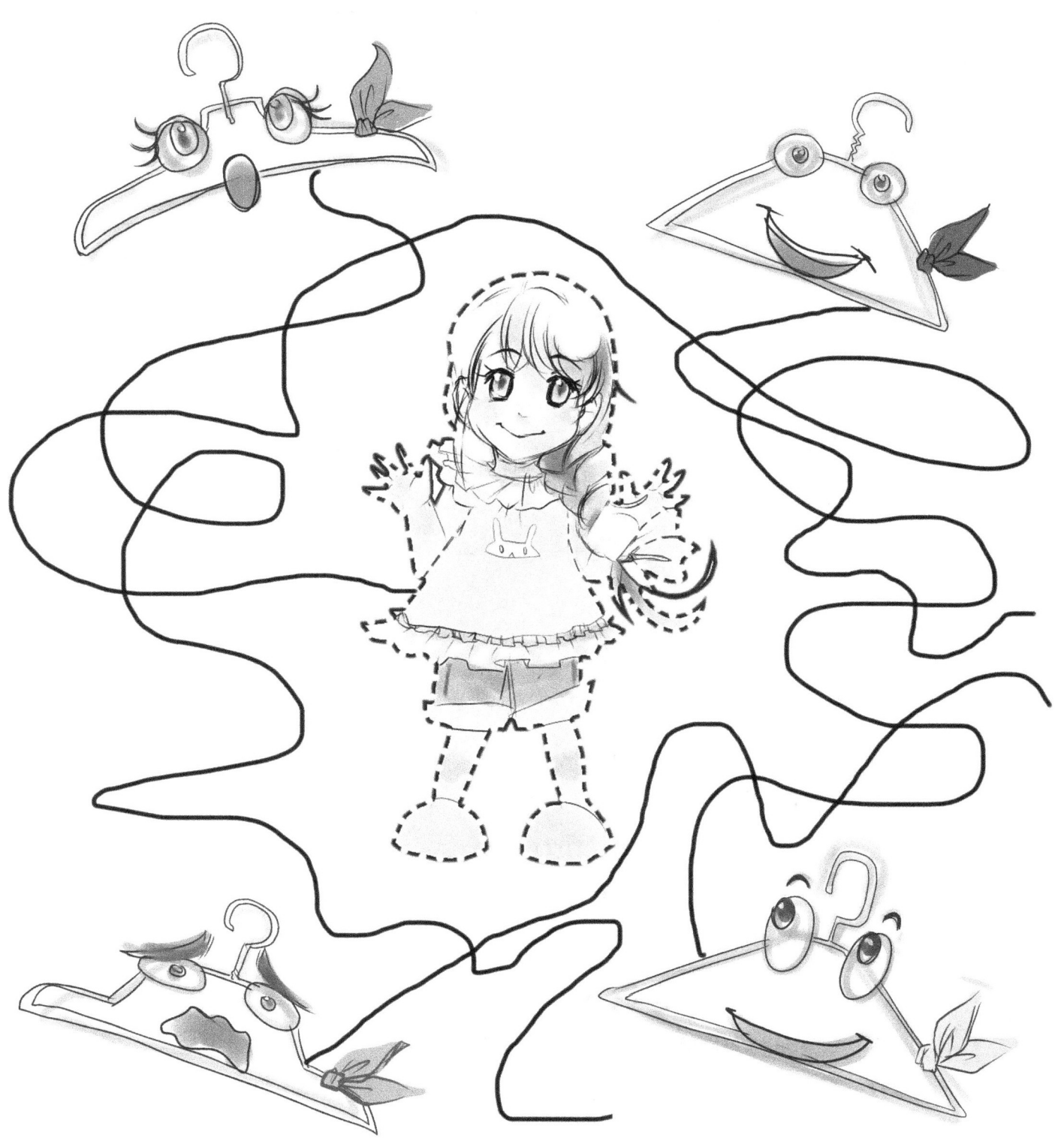

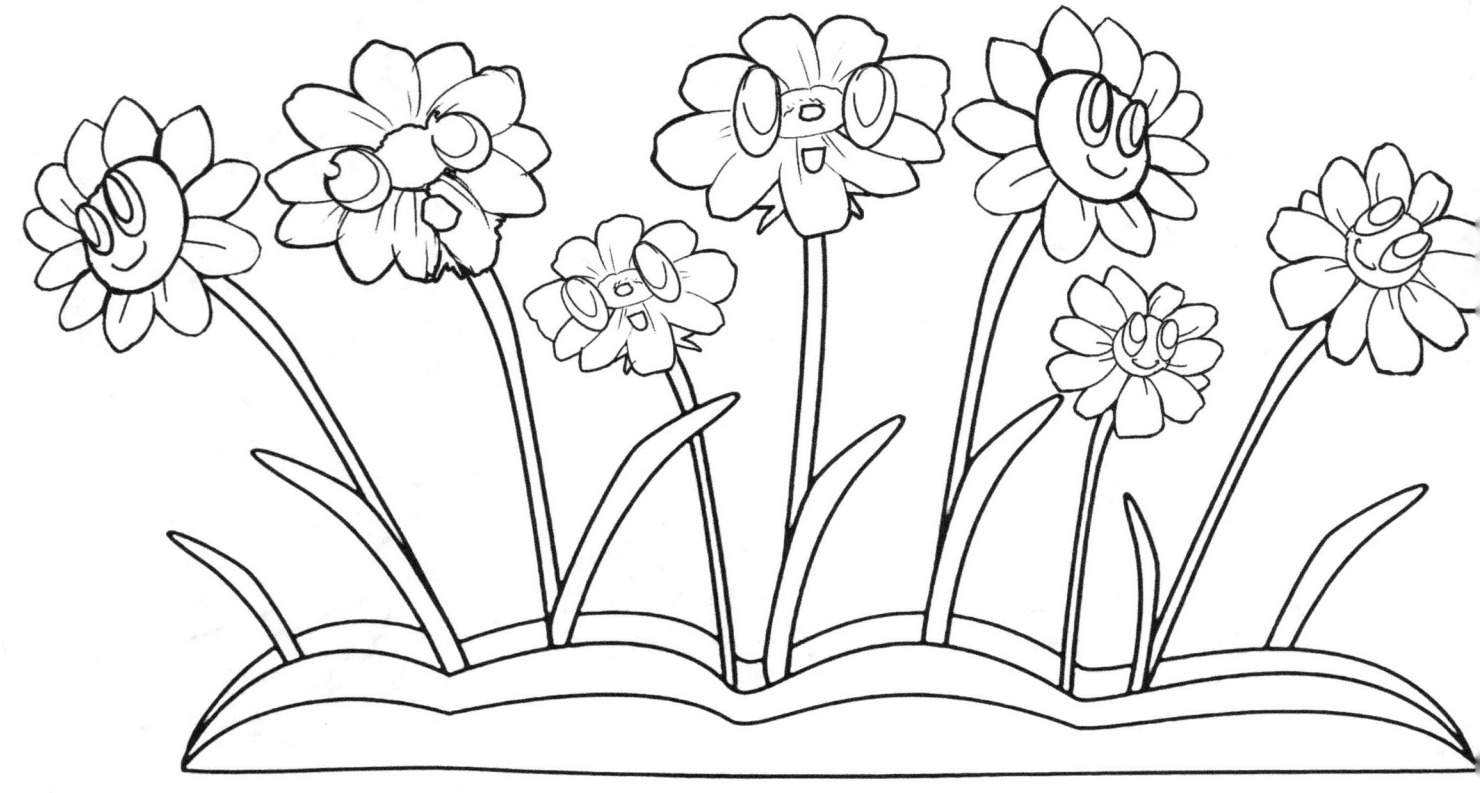

1. Color four leaves green.
2. Color three leaves yellow.
3. Color three stems orange.
4. Color two stems purple.
5. Color the ground brown.
6. Color the centers of three flowers red.
7. Color the centers of four flowers purple.
8. Color two flowers yellow.
9. Color three flowers orange.
10. Color two flowers blue.

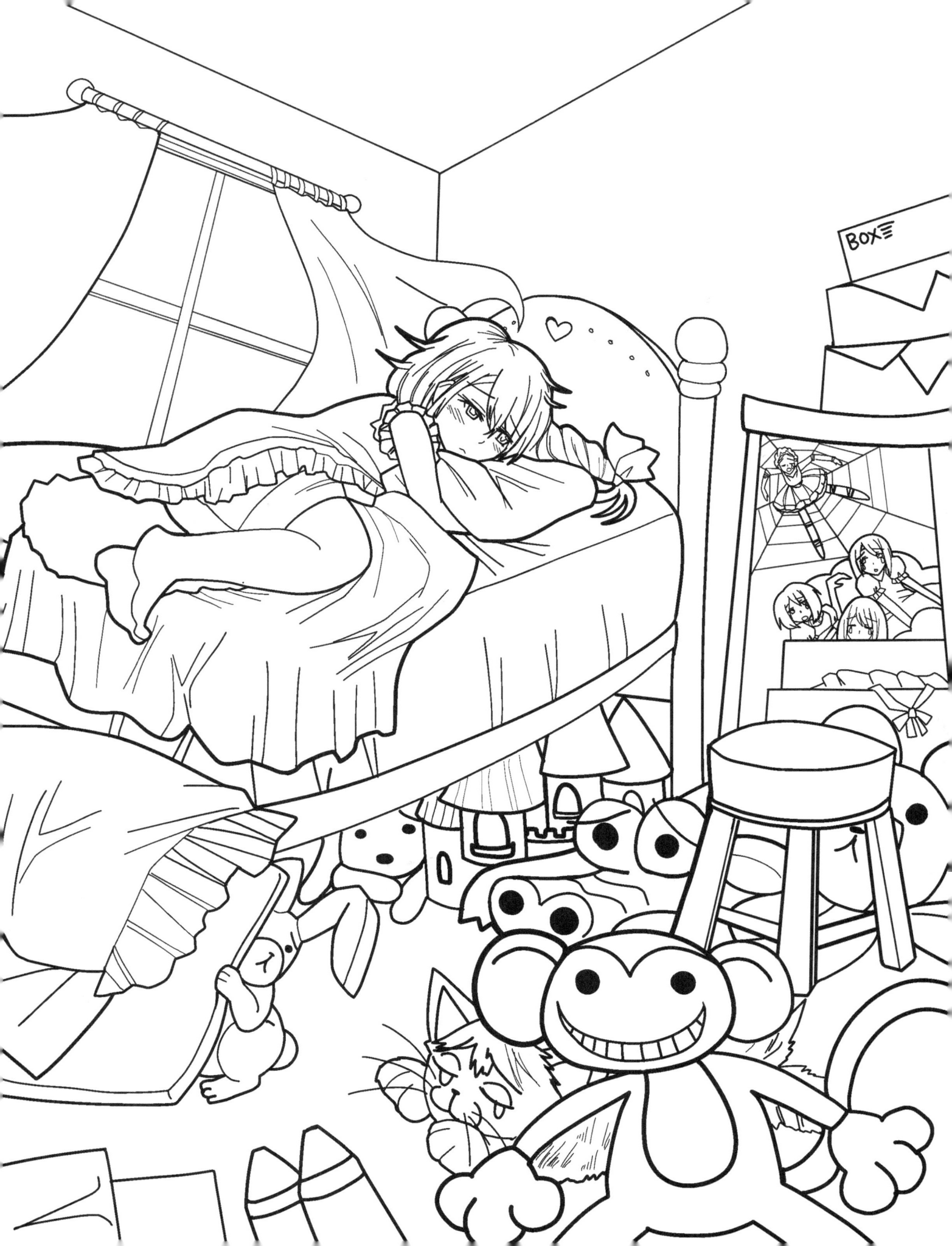

Design your socks with your favorite pictures!

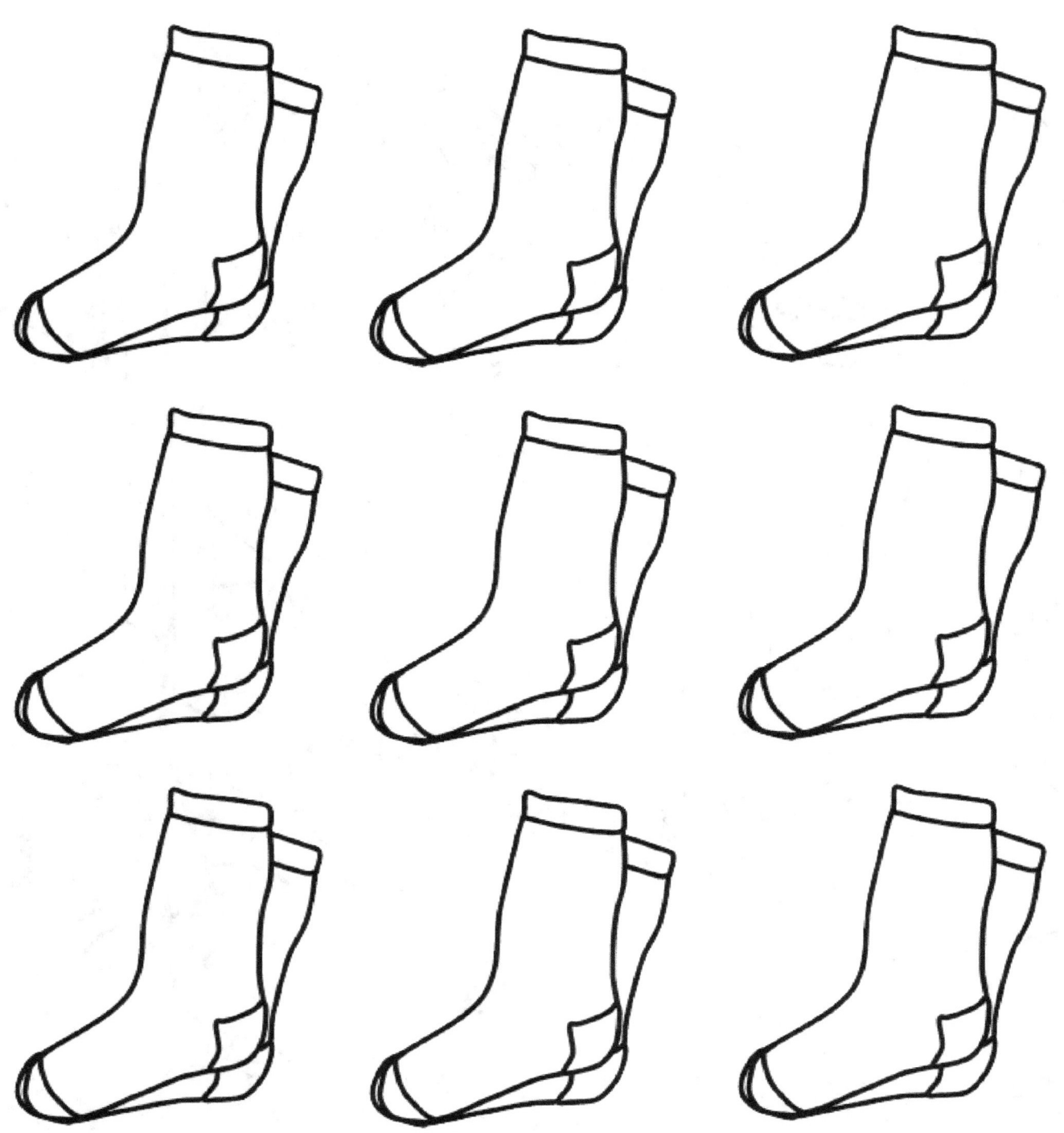

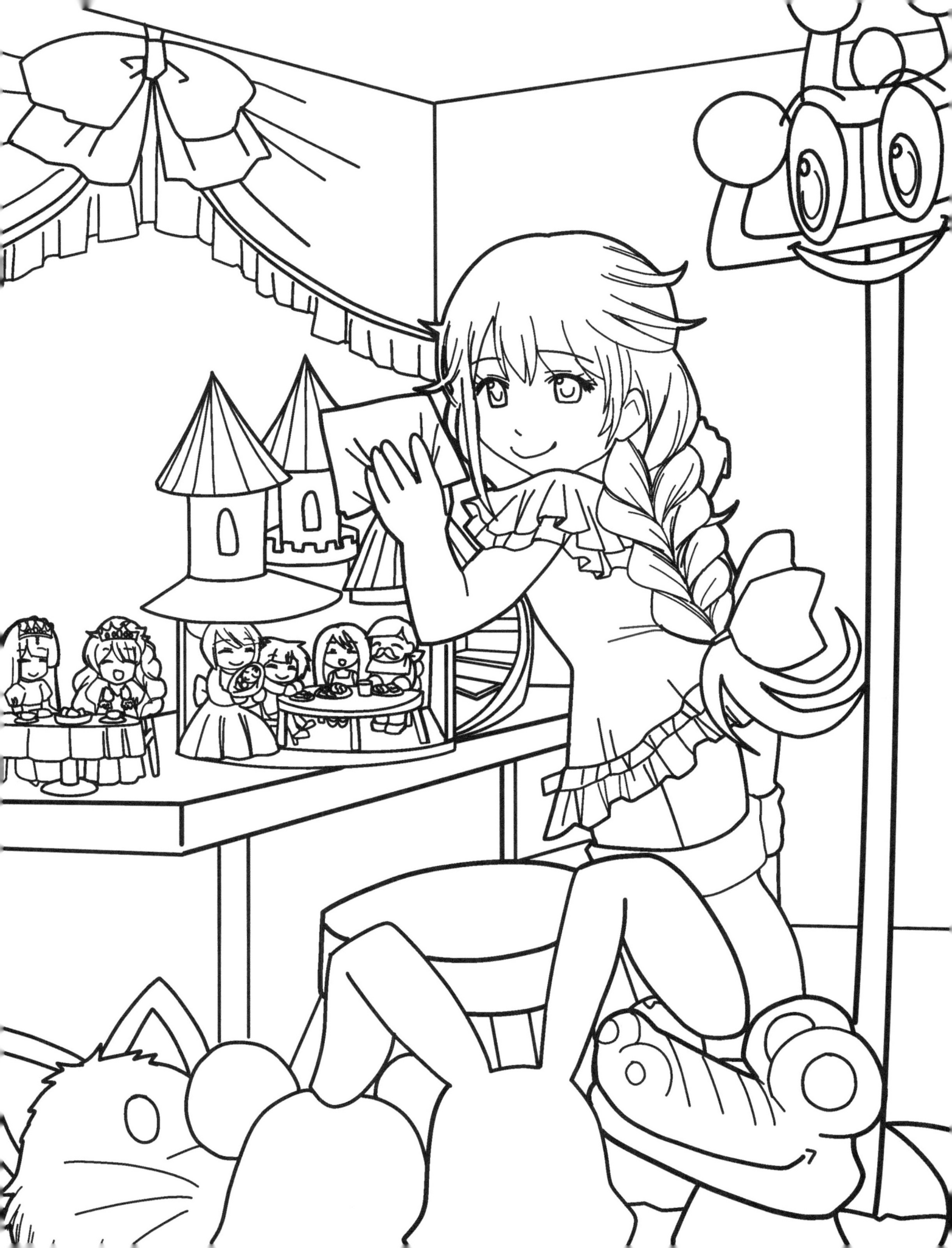

Name your favorite flowers and then color them.

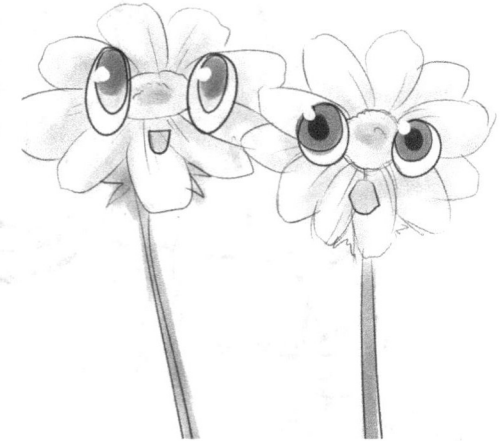

FLOWERS

_ _ _ _ _ _ _ _

_____

_____

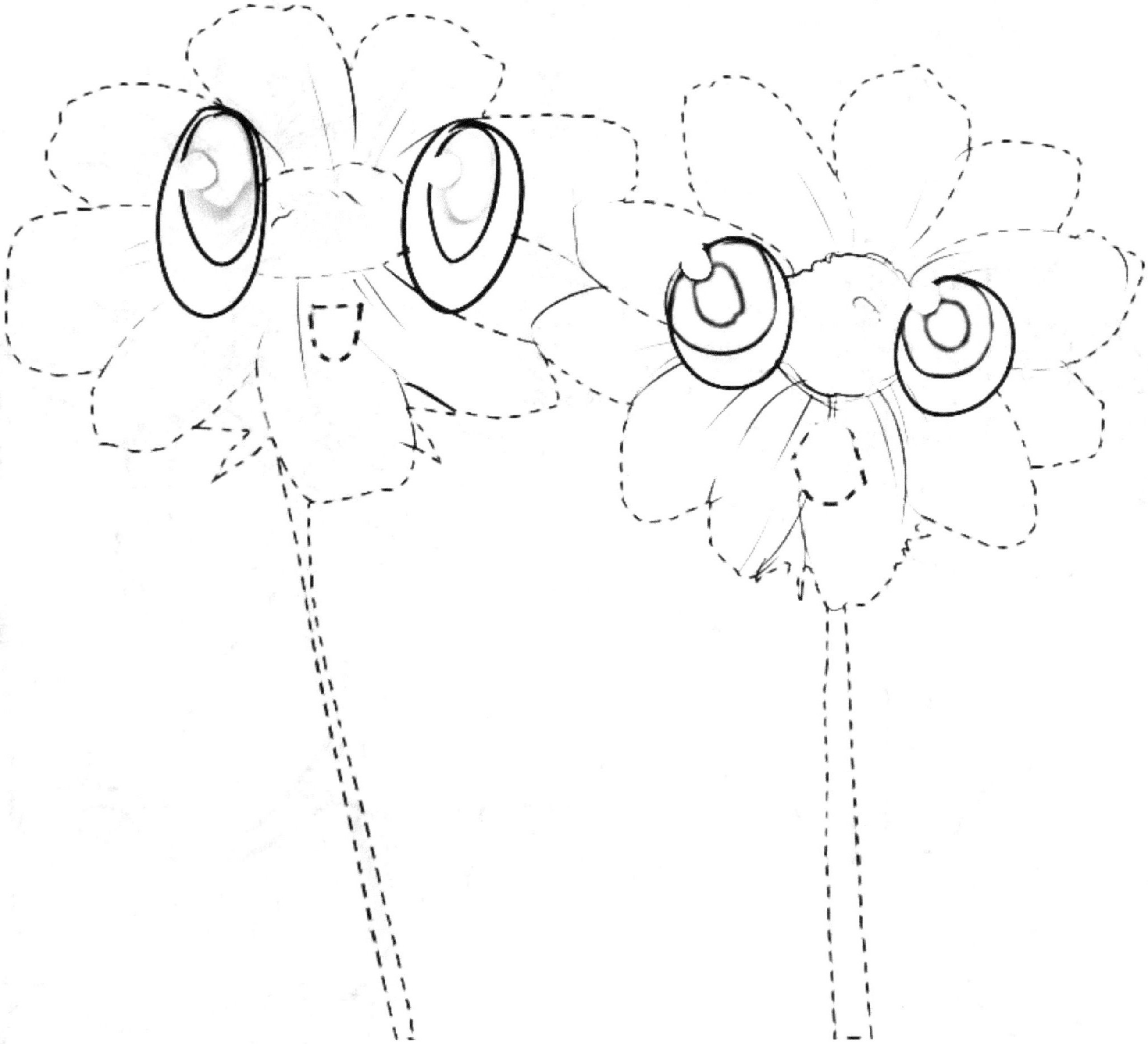

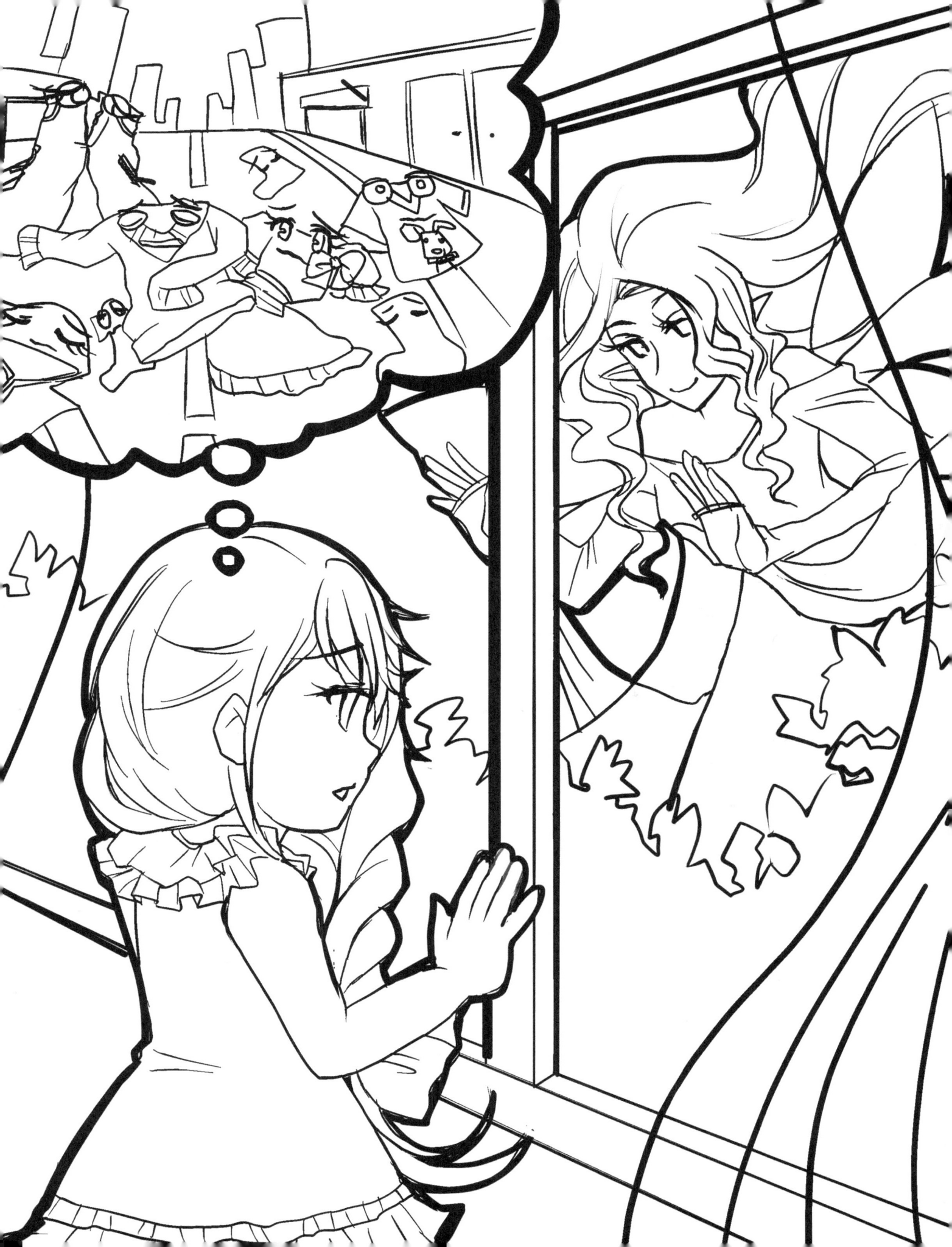

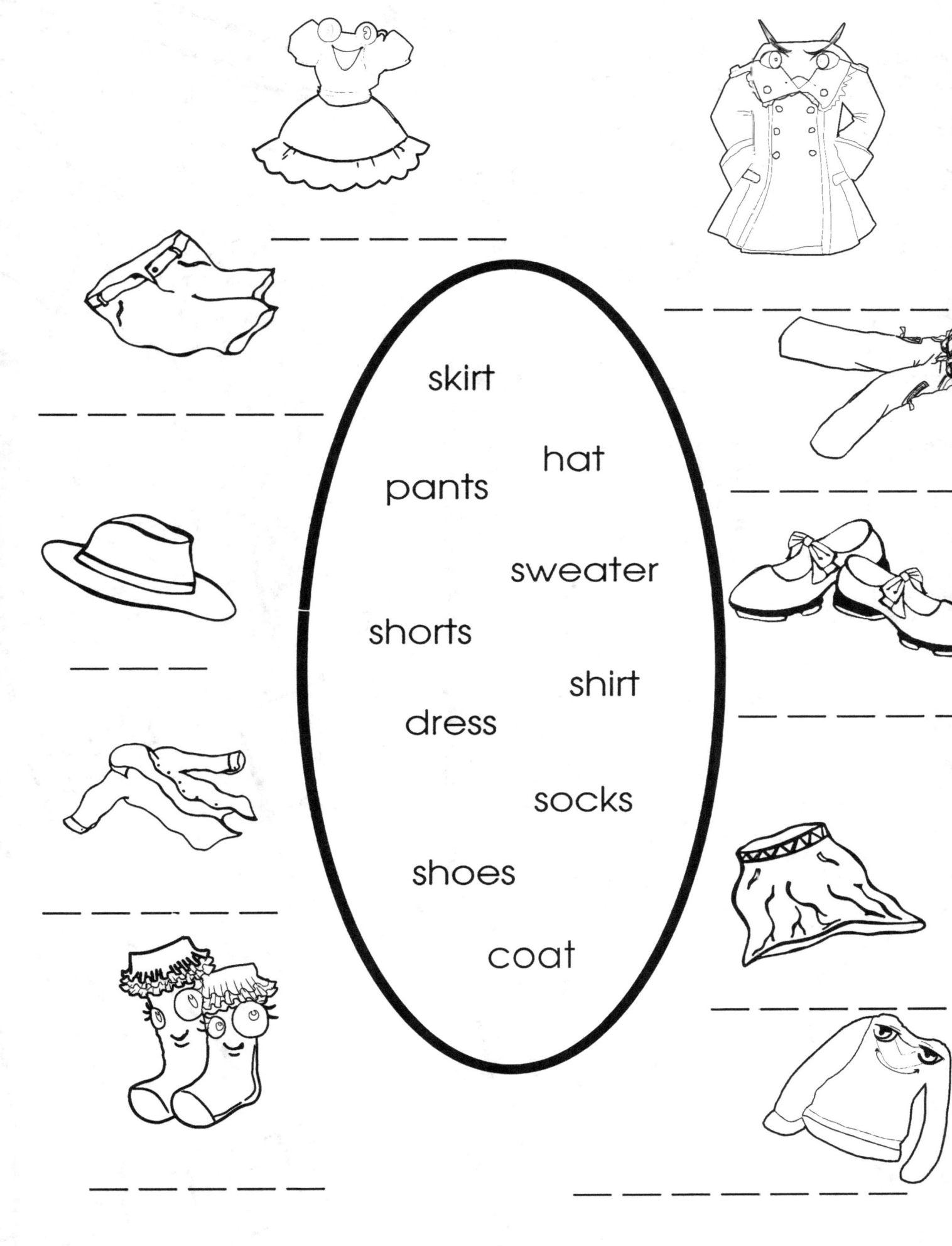

skirt

hat

pants

sweater

shorts

shirt

dress

socks

shoes

coat

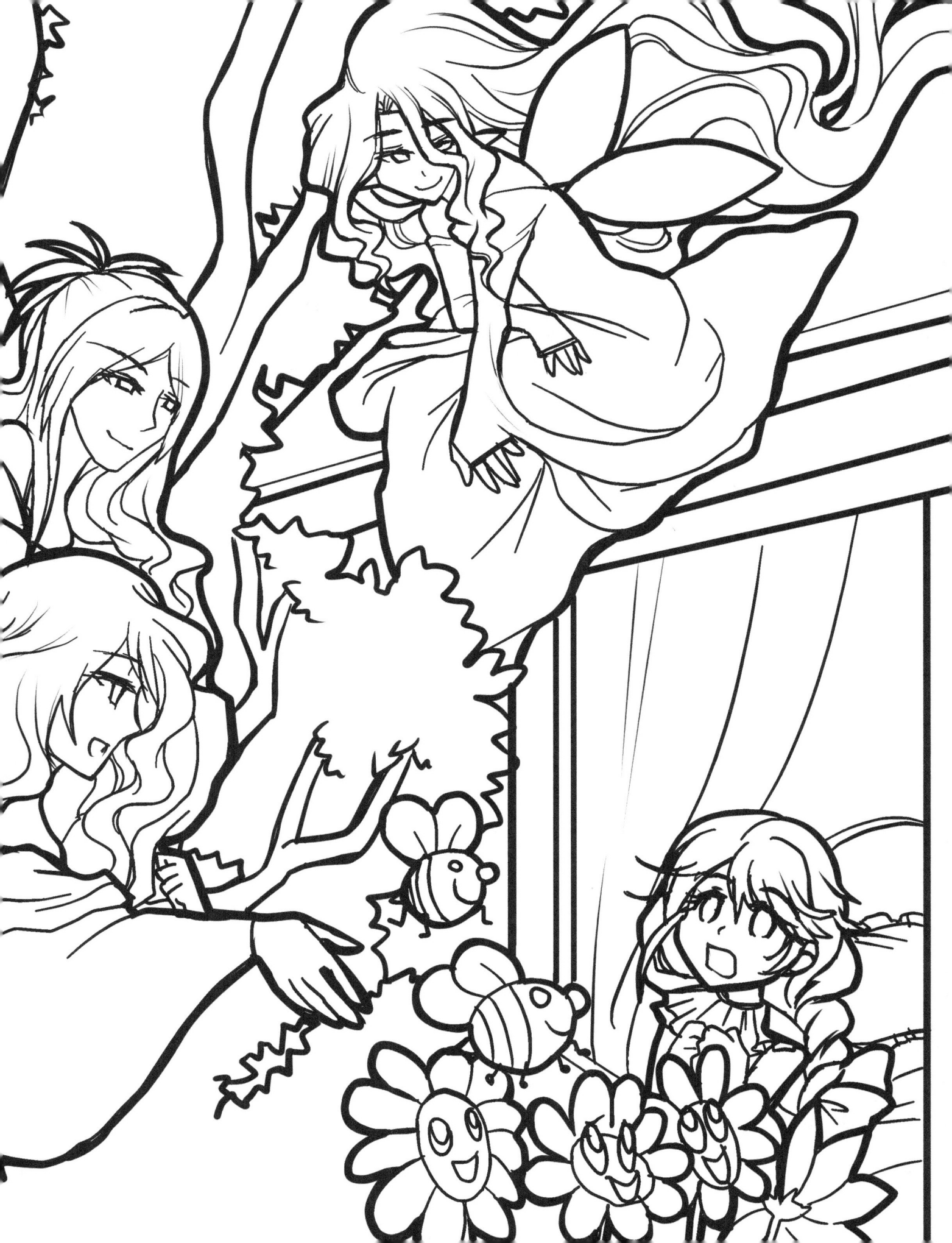

Design your own T-shirt - *just for fun!*

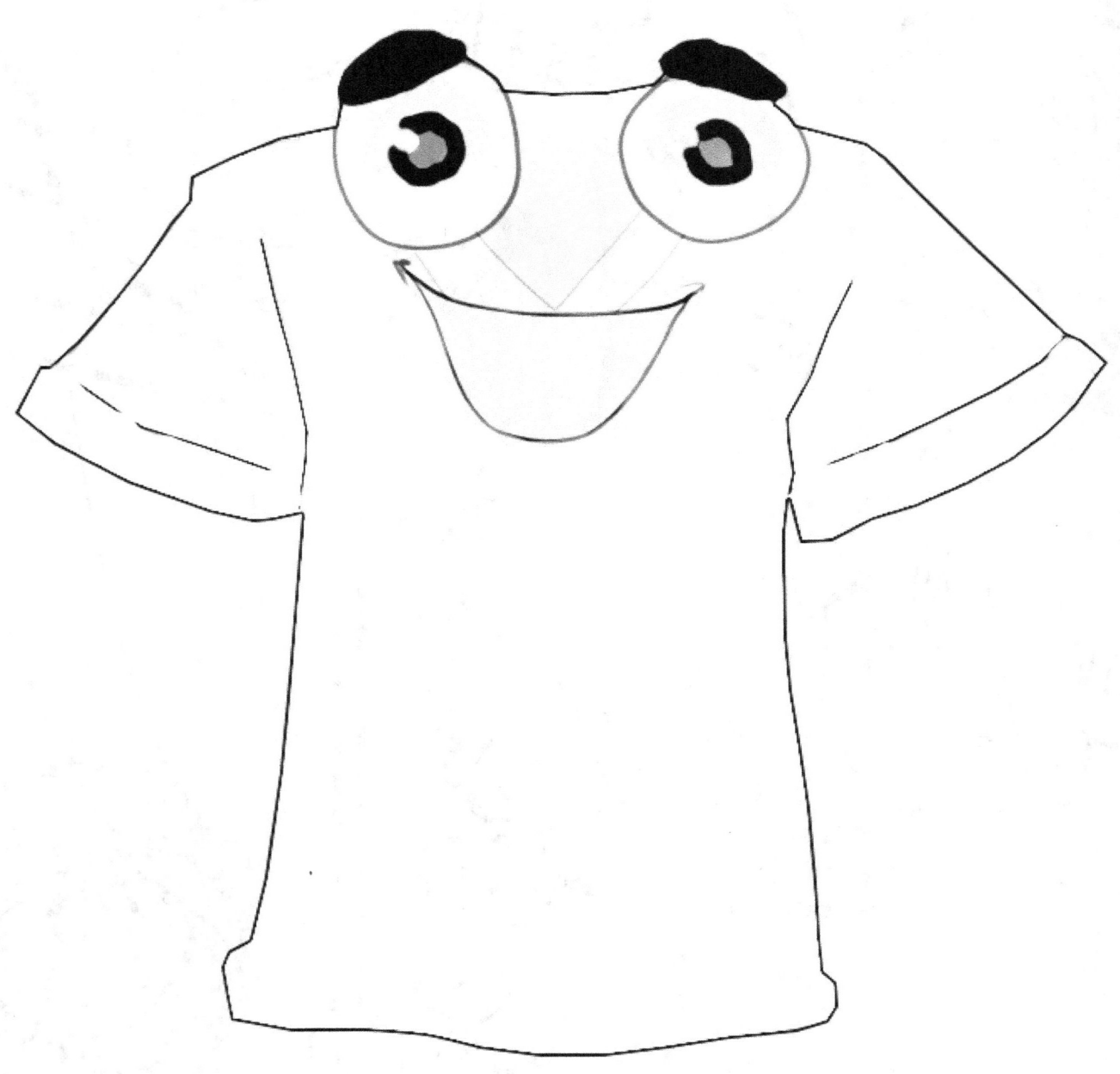

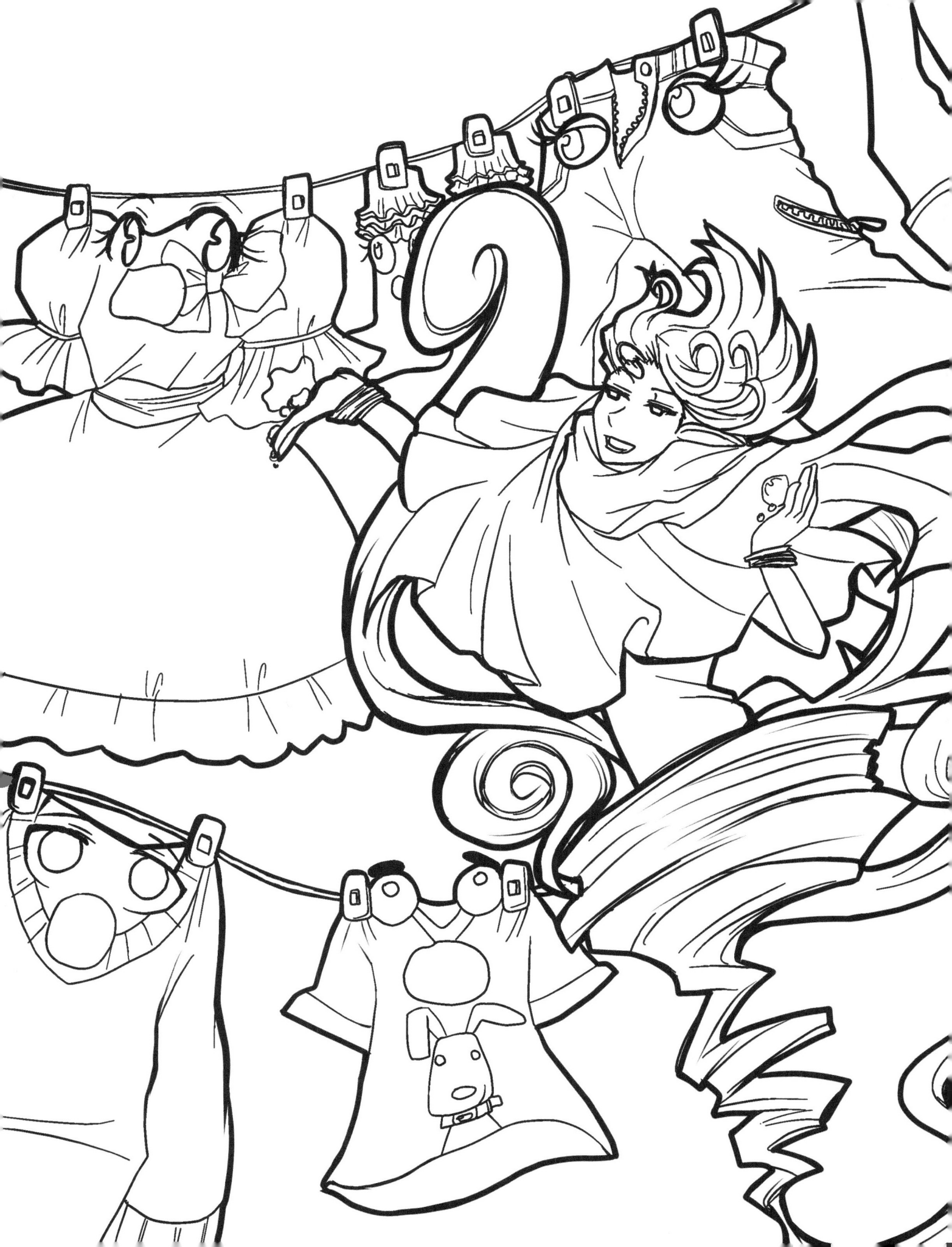

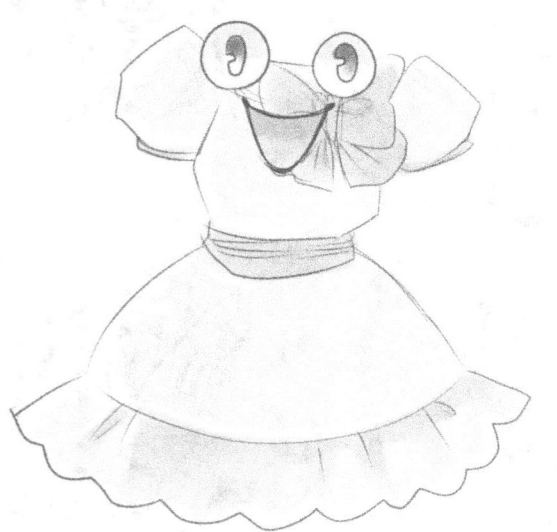

Color On!

DRESS

_ _ _ _ _

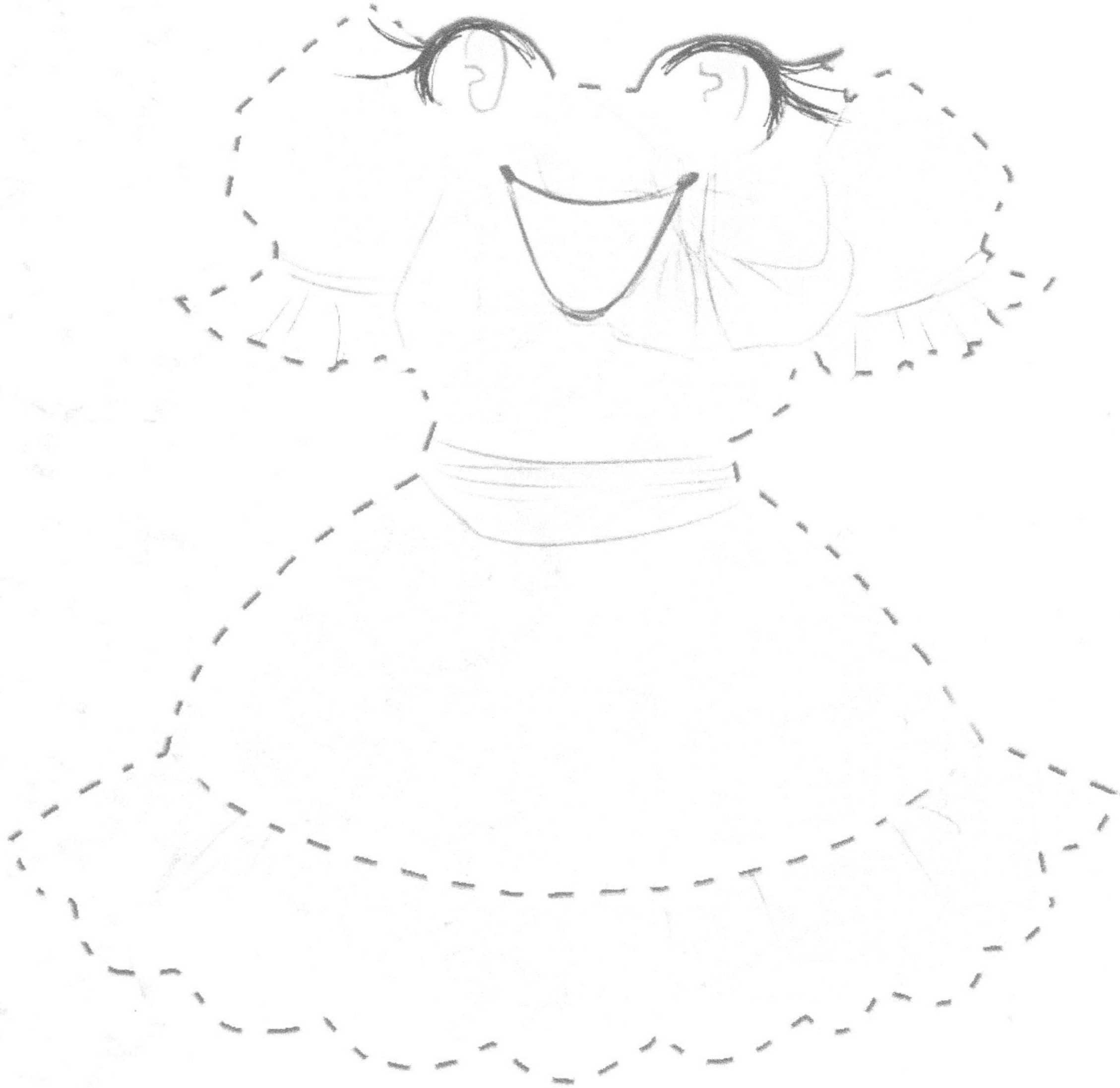

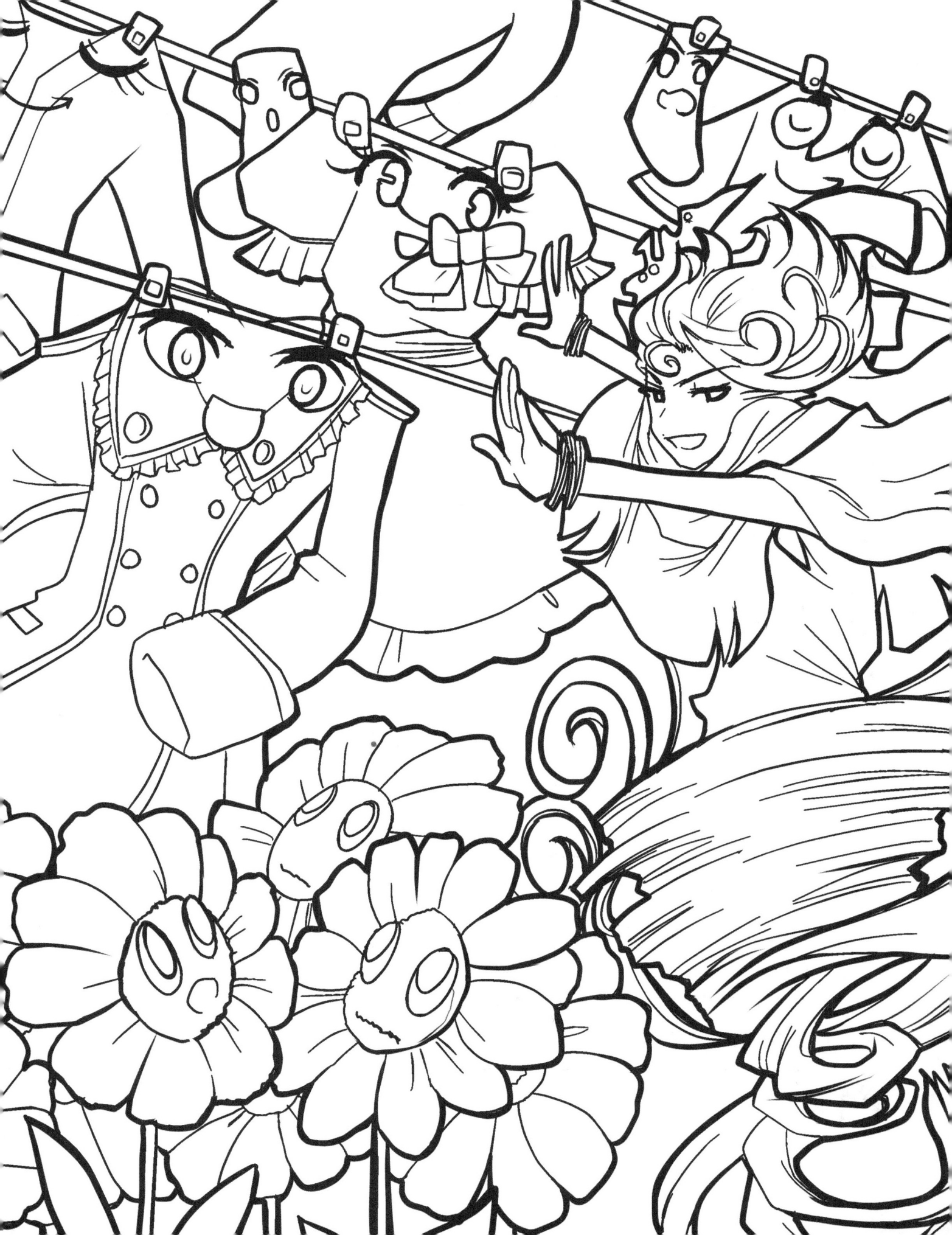

Clothing Vocabulary:
Clothes and Things We Wear!
There is no clothing in English that starts with X!

A Apron

B Boots

C Coat

D Dress

E Earmuffs

F Frock

G Gloves

H Hat

I Izar

J Jacket

K Kilt

L Leggings

M Mittens

N Negligee

O Overalls

P Pajamas

Q Quilted

R Robe

S Shoes

T T-Shirt

U Underwear

V Vest

W Waistcoat

X ~

Y Yarmulke

Z Zoot suit

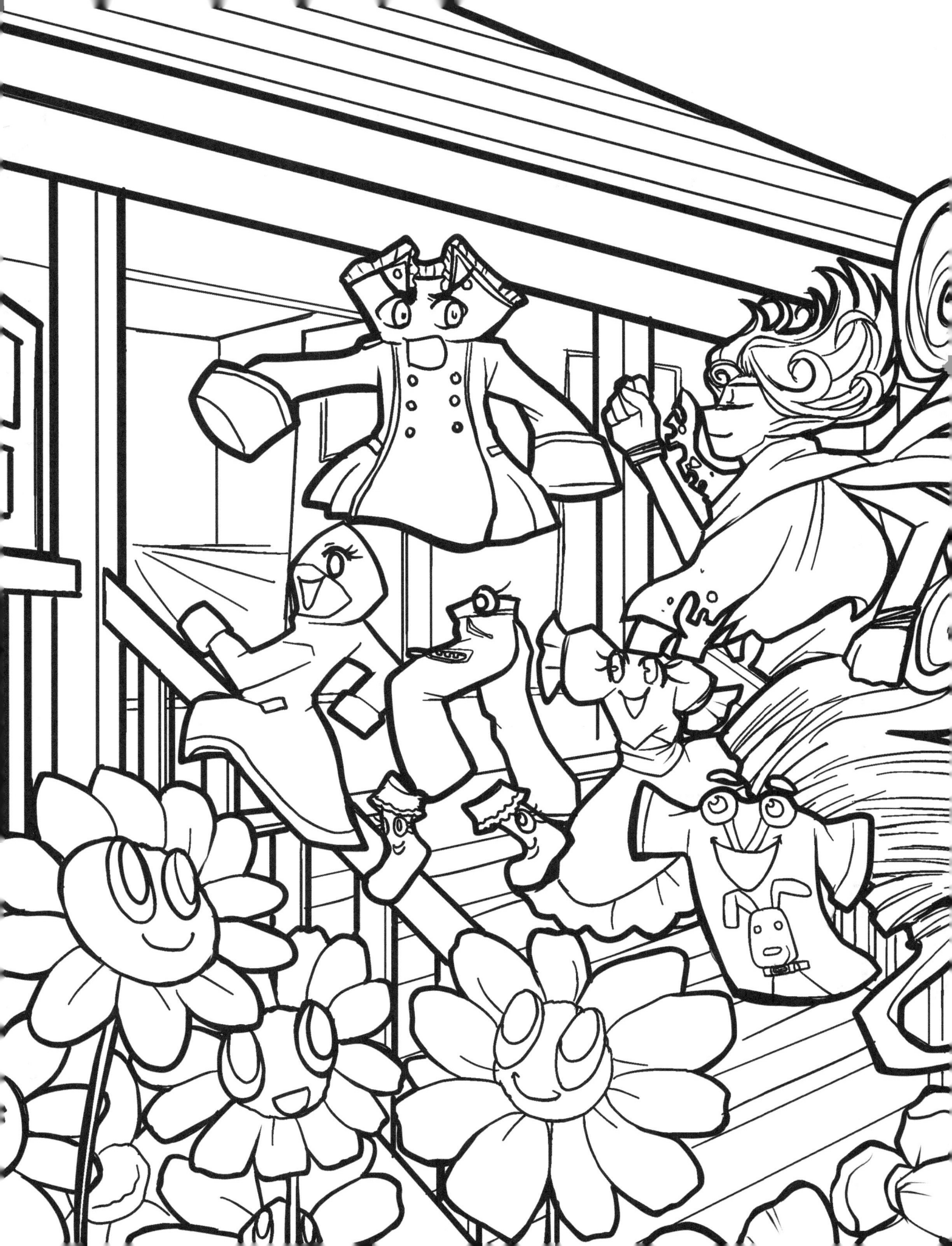

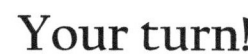

Your turn!

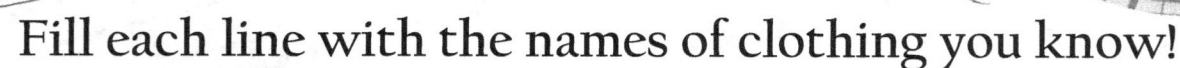

Fill each line with the names of clothing you know!

A	N
B	O
C	P
D	Q
E	R
F	S
G	T
H	U
I	V
J	W
K	X
L	Y
M	Z

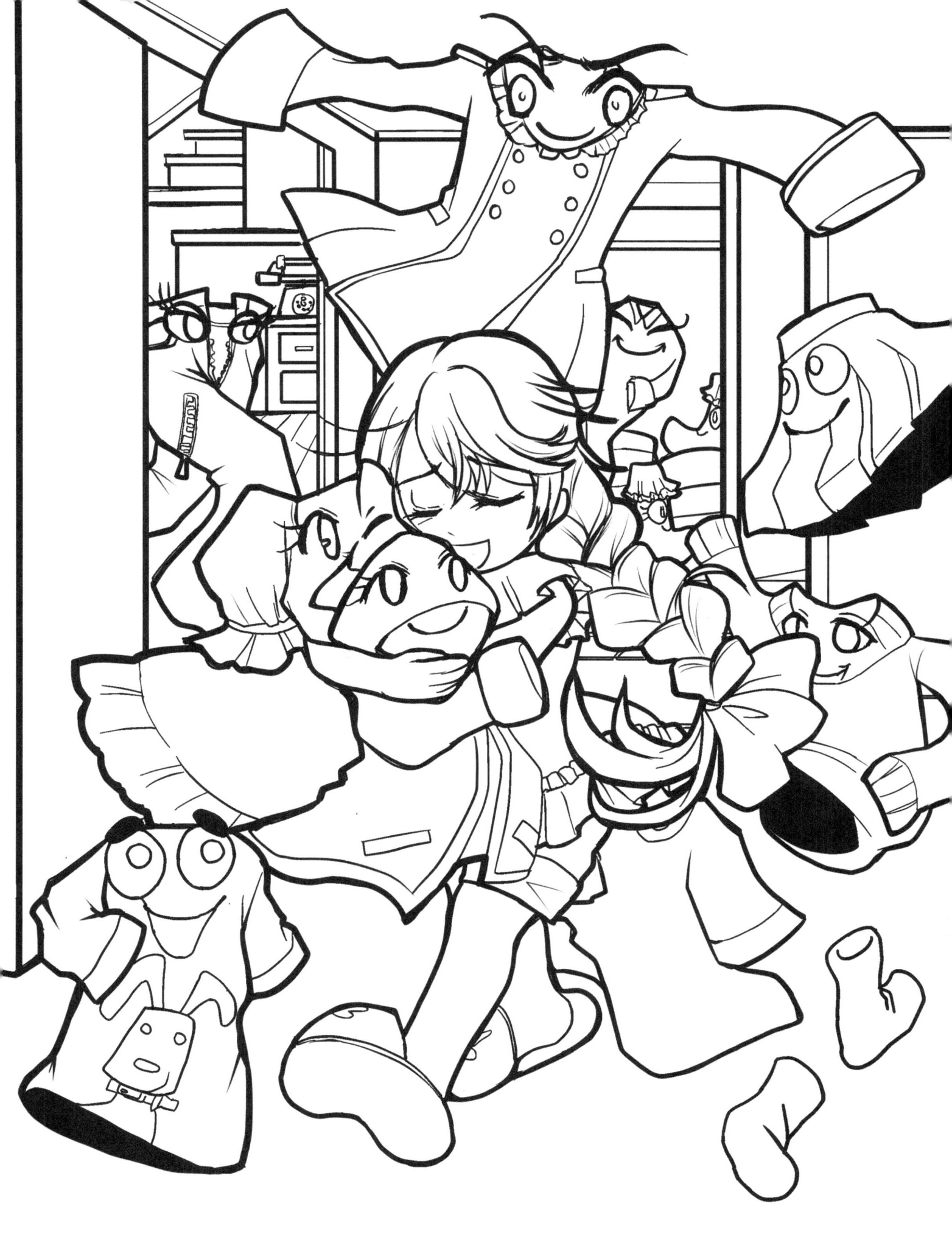

Write your own story and color!

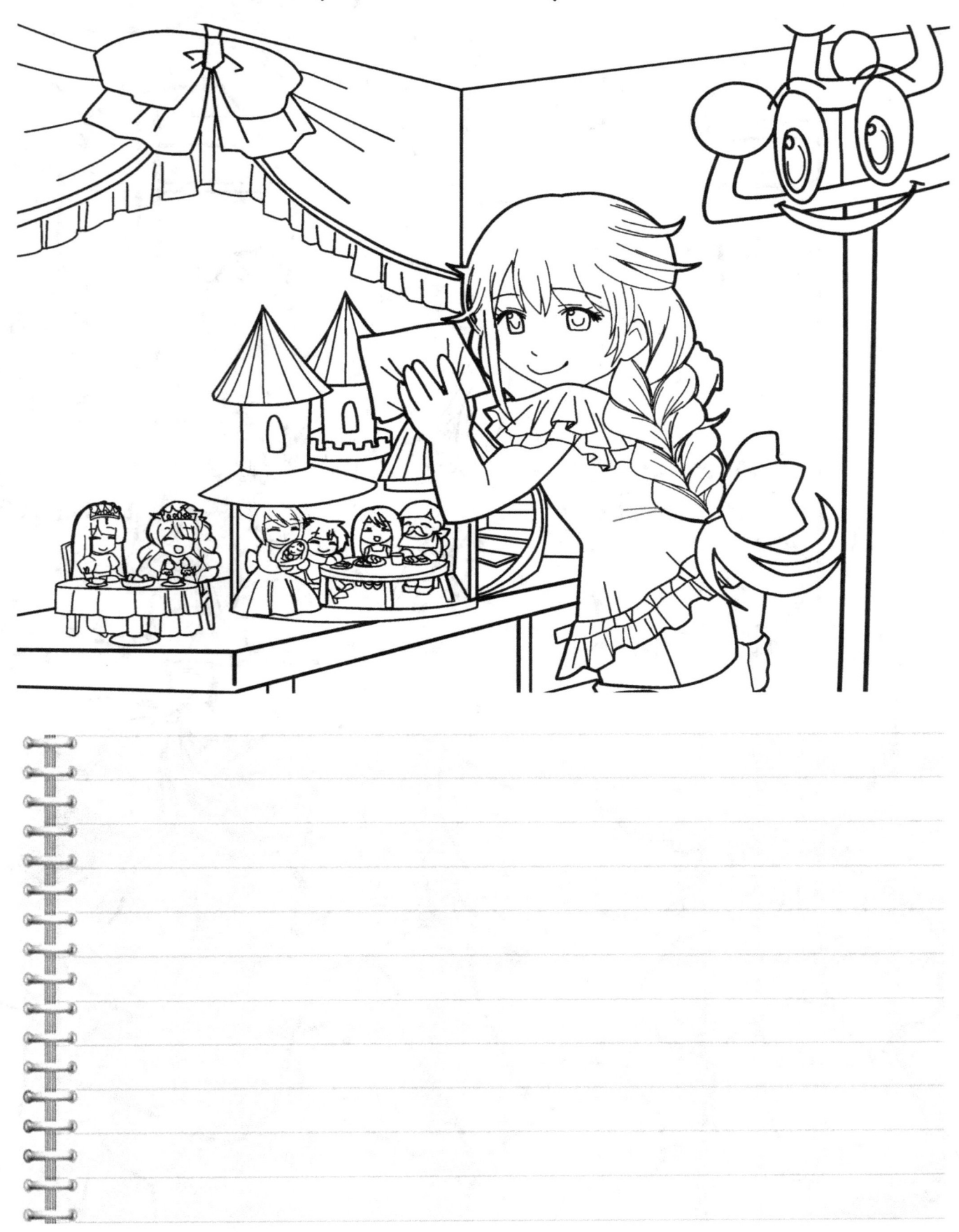

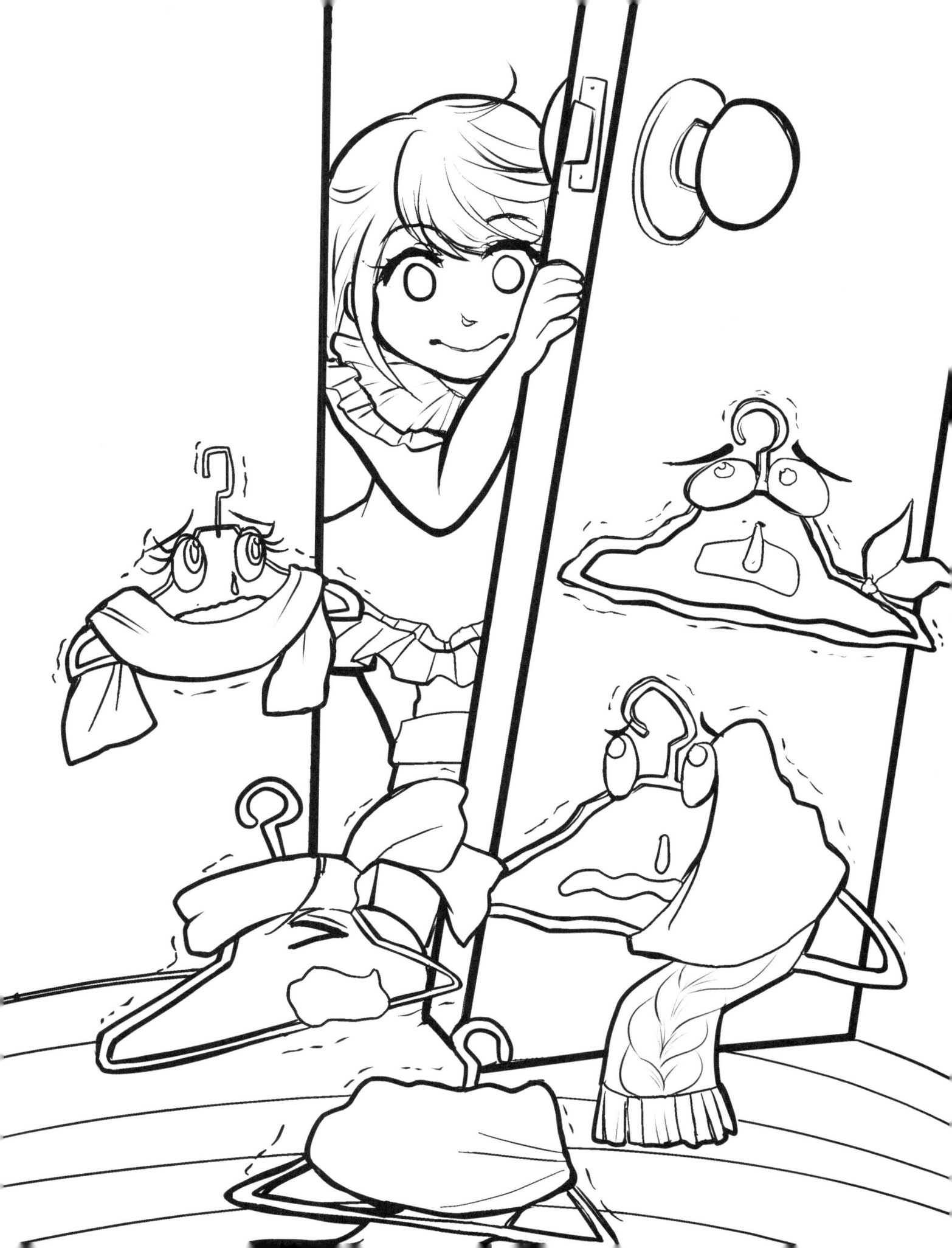

Clothing Match

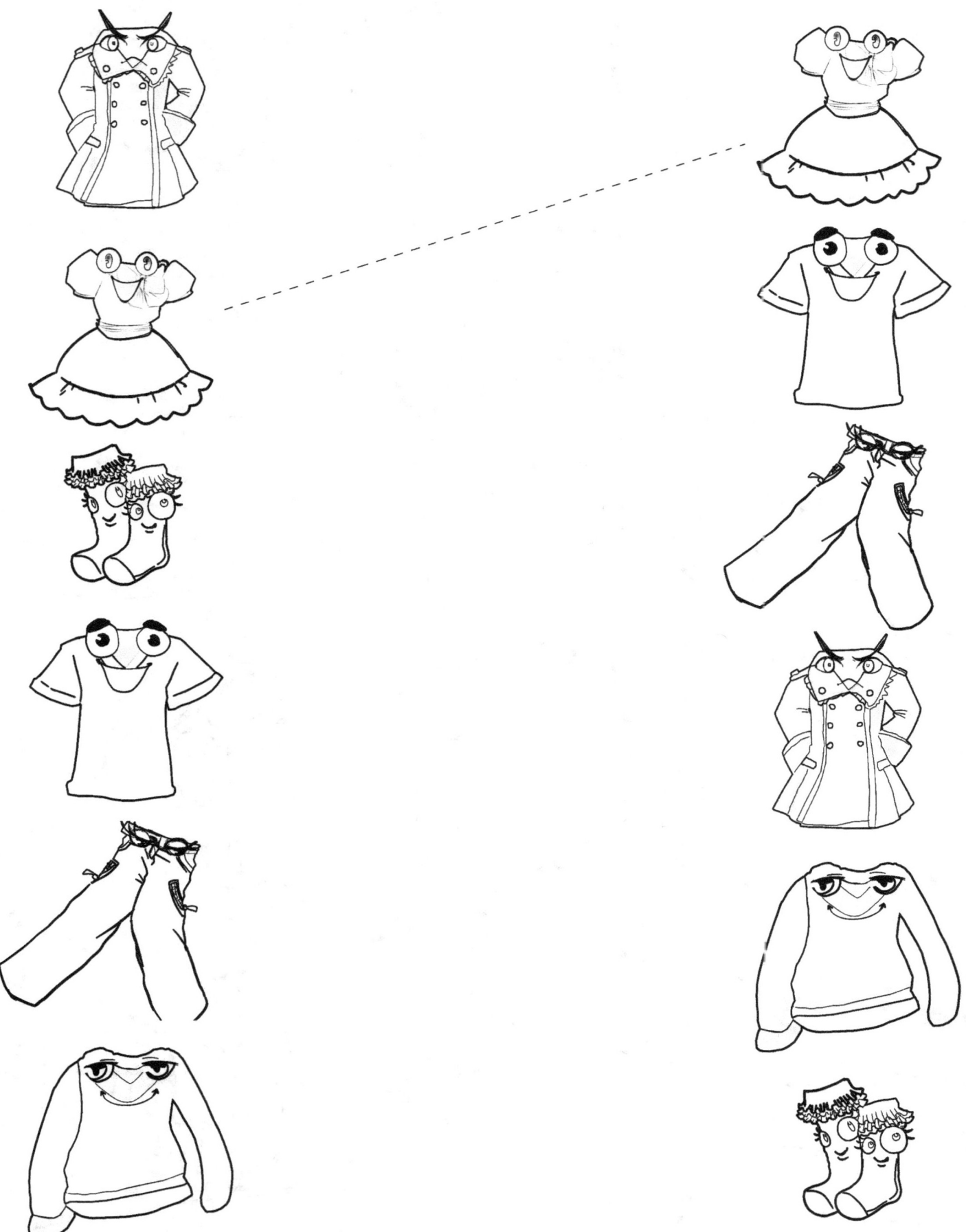

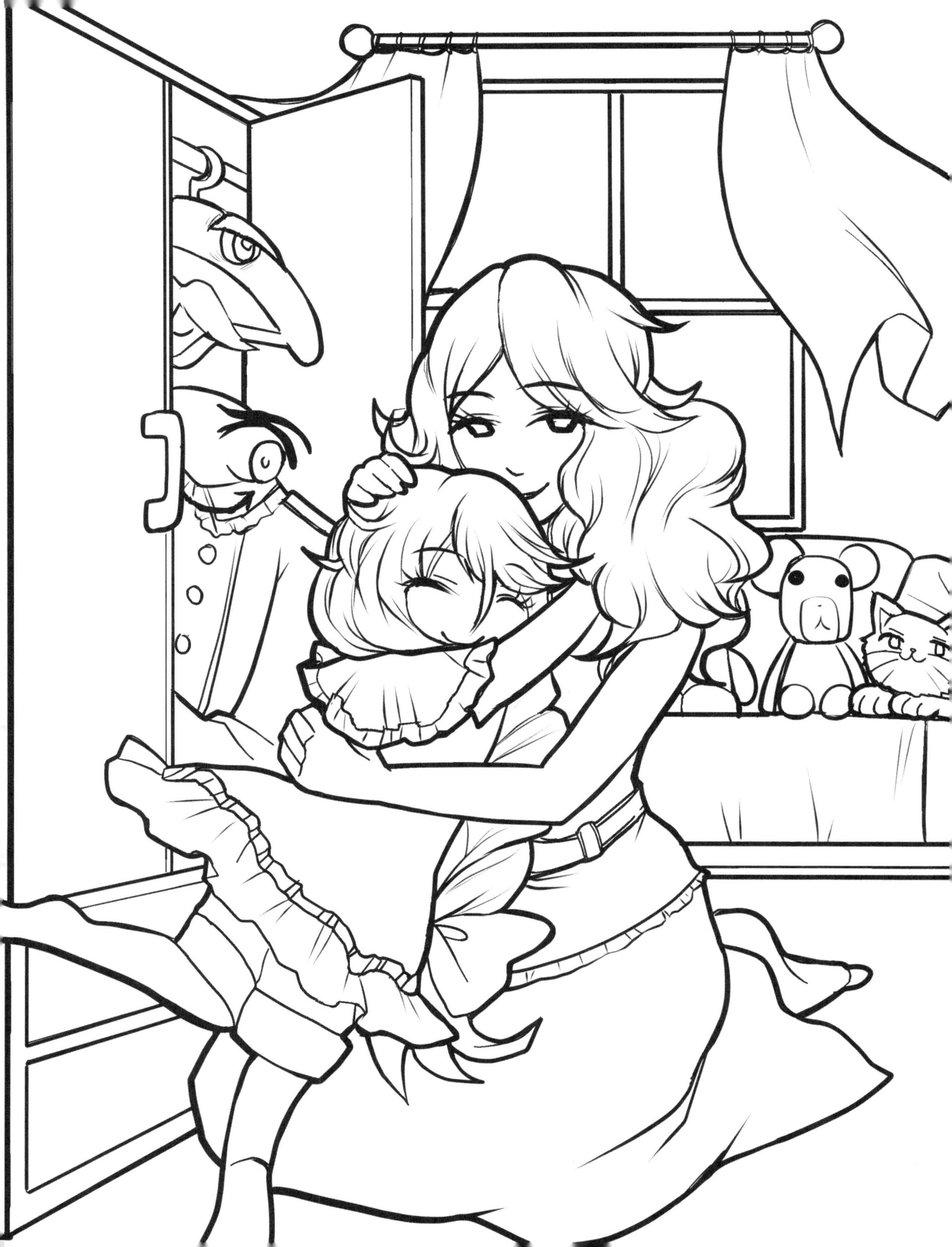

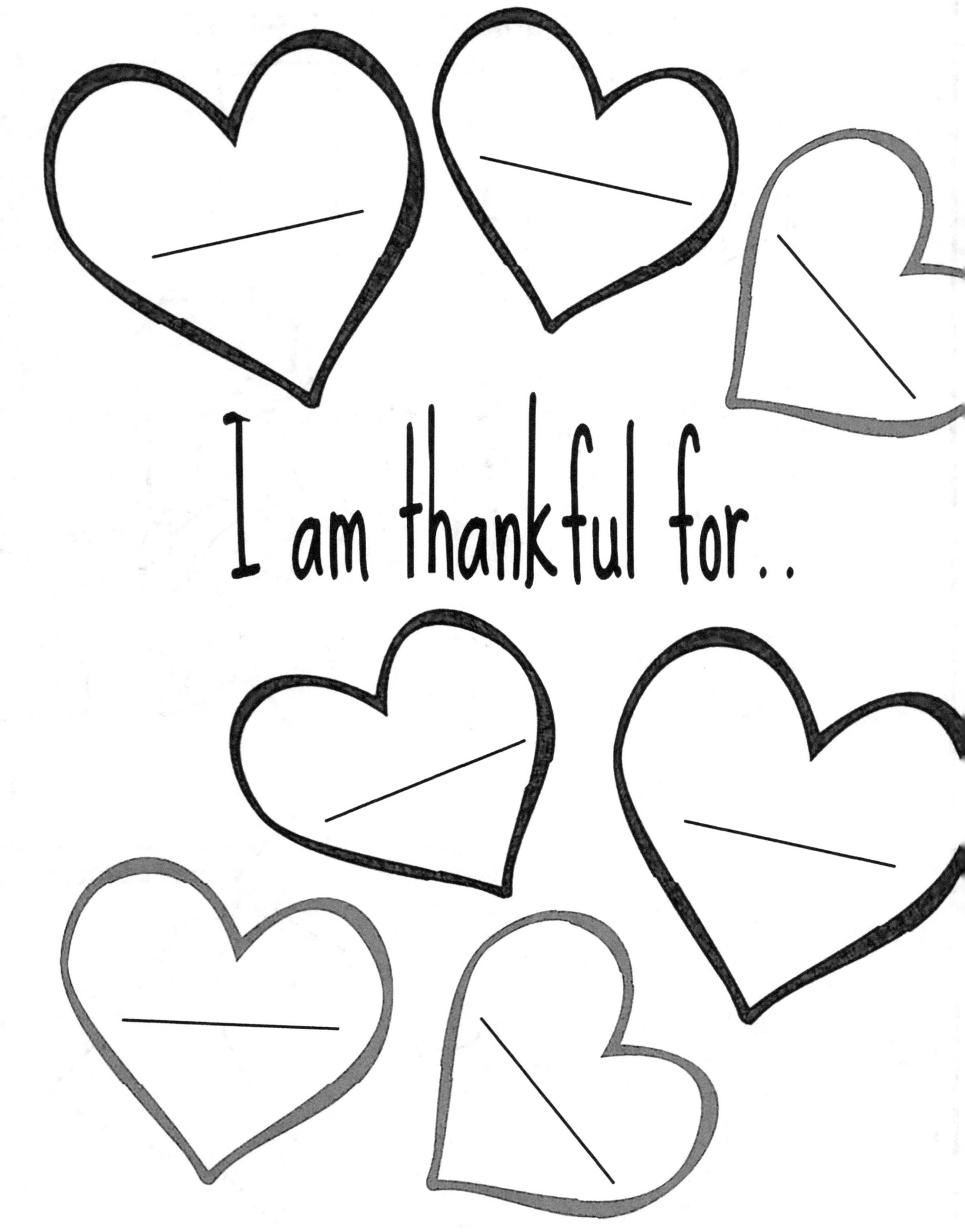

I am thankful for...

Closing Words

Memories of my children have always been my golden treasures when I write children's stories. Every time I dig out some event from my children's childhood, I discover something new, something I did not see in the past, something I overlooked. Now I can honestly say that over the years, the best lessons I learned were the ones that my children taught me. These lessons helped me to raise my girls into determined and ambitious young women, and I hope they will help other parents too.

Writing "Runaway Clothes," I saw a great opportunity to help families learn how to deal with an issue that drives every parent crazy. Going back in time, I always analyze my behavior and reactions that taught my children and me great lessons. Now, looking back on their mischievous misbehavior and the rules I tried to apply, I see things that I wish I had done differently. Like many parents, I naively thought I would have perfect children, just as I saw on the front page of parenting magazines—happy, smart, and well-behaved. The reality proved me wrong. There is no perfect child or parent. Parents and children learn from each other on a daily basis. Raising my girls, I learned that not every rule is written in stone, and that sometimes, unplanned lessons are the best teachers.

The older I get, the more memories I collect. Some of them vanish with time, but some never leave. Happy or sad, funny or disappointing, they are part of my life and my stories. With age, I grew wiser and looked at things differently. The stuff that once drove me crazy and seemed so important then, appears funny now. As my grandfather would say, learn as you live.

I recommend "Runaway Clothes" to school classrooms, library circles, and parents who wish to read a lovely tale with a moral about taking care of our belongings, to children ages 5 to 10.

COLOR ON and READ A LOT! And of course do not forget to clean your room, kids. Remember, clothes have feelings also!